HAWTHORNE'S
THE SCARLET LETTER

Other books in the Christian Guides to the Classics Series:

HAWTHORNE'S
THE SCARLET LETTER

LELAND RYKEN

CROSSWAY
WHEATON, ILLINOIS

Hawthorne's "The Scarlet Letter"

Copyright © 2013 by Leland Ryken

Published by Crossway
    1300 Crescent Street
    Wheaton, Illinois 60187

Cover illustration: Howell Golson

Cover design: Simplicated Studio

First printing 2013

Printed in the United States of America

Trade paperback ISBN: 978-1-4335-2608-4
PDF ISBN: 978-1-4335-2609-1
Mobipocket ISBN: 978-1-4335-2610-7
ePub ISBN: 978-1-4335-2611-4

Library of Congress Cataloging-in-Publication Data

Ryken, Leland.
    Hawthorne's The Scarlet Letter / Leland Ryken.
        p.   cm.— (Christian guides to the classics)
    ISBN 978-1-4335-2608-4 (tp)
        1. Hawthorne, Nathaniel, 1804-1864. Scarlet letter.
    2. Christianity and literature. I. Title.
PS1868.R95   2013
813'.3—dc23   2012025869

BP		23	22	21	20	19	18	17	16	15	14	13
15	14	13	12	11	10	9	8	7	6	5	4	3	2	1

Contents

The Nature and Function of Literature

We need to approach any piece of writing with the right expectations, based on the kind of writing that it is. The expectations that we should bring to any work of literature are the following.

The subject of literature. The subject of literature is human experience, rendered as concretely as possible. Literature should thus be contrasted to expository writing of the type we use to conduct the ordinary business of life. Literature does not aim to impart facts and information. It exists to make us share a series of experiences. Literature appeals to our image-making and image-perceiving capacity. A famous novelist said that his purpose was to make his readers *see*, by which he meant to see life.

The universality of literature. To take that one step further, the subject of literature is *universal* human experience—what is true for all people at all times in all places. This does not contradict the fact that literature is first of all filled with concrete particulars. The particulars of literature are a net whereby the author captures and expresses the universal. History and the daily news tell us what *happened*; literature tells us what *happens*. The task that this imposes on us is to recognize and name the familiar experiences that we vicariously live as we read a work of literature. The truth that literature imparts is truthfulness to life—knowledge in the form of seeing things accurately. As readers we not only look *at* the world of the text but *through* it to everyday life.

An interpretation of life. In addition to portraying human experiences, authors give us their interpretation of those experiences. There is a persuasive aspect to literature, as authors attempt to get us to share their views of life. These interpretations of life can be phrased as ideas or themes. An important part of assimilating imaginative literature is thus determining and evaluating an author's angle of vision and belief system.

The importance of literary form. A further aspect of literature arises from the fact that authors are artists. They write in distinctly literary genres such as narrative and poetry. Additionally, literary authors want us to share their love of technique and beauty, all the way from skill with words to an ability to structure a work carefully and artistically.

Summary. A work of imaginative literature aims to make us see life accurately, to get us to think about important ideas, and to enjoy an artistic performance.

Why the Classics Matter

This book belongs to a series of guides to the literary classics of Western literature. We live at a time when the concept of a literary classic is often misunderstood and when the classics themselves are often undervalued or even attacked. The very concept of a classic will rise in our estimation if we simply understand what it is.

What is a classic? To begin, the term *classic* implies the best in its class. The first hurdle that a classic needs to pass is excellence. Excellent according to whom? This brings us to a second part of our definition: classics have stood the test of time through the centuries. The human race itself determines what works rise to the status of classics. That needs to be qualified slightly: the classics are especially known and valued by people who have received a formal education, alerting us that the classics form an important part of the education that takes place within a culture.

This leads us to yet another aspect of classics: classics are known to us not only in themselves but also in terms of their interpretation and reinterpretation through the ages. We know a classic partly in terms of the attitudes and interpretations that have become attached to it through the centuries.

Why read the classics? The first good reason to read the classics is that they represent the best. The fact that they are difficult to read is a mark in their favor; within certain limits, of course, works of literature that demand a lot from us will always yield more than works that demand little of us. If we have a taste for what is excellent, we will automatically want some contact with classics. They offer more enjoyment, more understanding about human experience, and more richness of ideas and thought than lesser works (which we can also legitimately read). We finish reading or rereading a classic with a sense of having risen higher than we would otherwise have risen.

Additionally, to know the classics is to know the past, and with that knowledge comes a type of power and mastery. If we know the past, we are in some measure protected from the limitations that come when all we know is the contemporary. Finally, to know the classics is to be an educated person. Not to know them is, intellectually and culturally speaking, like walking around without an arm or leg.

Summary. Here are four definitions of a literary classic from literary experts; each one provides an angle on why the classics matter. (1) The best that has been thought and said (Matthew Arnold). (2) "A literary classic ranks with the best of its kind that have been produced" (*Harper Handbook to Literature*). (3) A classic "lays its images permanently on the mind [and] is entirely irreplaceable in the sense that no other book whatever comes anywhere near reminding you of it or being even a momentary substitute for it" (C. S. Lewis). (4) Classics are works to which "we return time and again in our minds, even if we do not reread them frequently, as touchstones by which we interpret the world around us" (Nina Baym).

How to Read a Story

The Scarlet Letter, like the other classics discussed in this series, is a narrative or story. To read it with enjoyment and understanding, we need to know how stories work and why people write and read them.

Why do people tell and read stories? To tell a story is to (a) entertain and (b) make a statement. As for the entertainment value of stories, it is a fact that one of the most universal human impulses can be summed up in the four words *tell me a story*. The appeal of stories is universal, and all of us are incessant storytellers during the course of a typical day. As for *making a statement*, a novelist hit the nail on the head when he said that in order for storytellers to tell a story they must have some picture of the world and of what is right and wrong in that world.

The things that make up a story. All stories are comprised of three things that claim our attention—setting, character, and plot. A good story is a balance among these three. In one sense, storytellers tell us *about* these things, but in another sense, as fiction writer Flannery O'Connor put it, storytellers don't speak *about* plot, setting, and character but *with* them. *About what* does the storyteller tell us by means of these things? About life, human experience, and the ideas that the storyteller believes to be true.

World making as part of storytelling. To read a story is to enter a whole world of the imagination. Storytellers construct their narrative world carefully. World making is a central part of the storyteller's enterprise. On the one hand, this is part of what makes stories entertaining. We love to be transported from mundane reality to faraway places with strange-sounding names. But storytellers also intend their imagined worlds as accurate pictures of reality. In other words, it is an important part of the truth claims that they intend to make. Accordingly, we need to pay attention to the details of the world that a storyteller creates, viewing that world as a picture of what the author believes to exist.

The need to be discerning. The first demand that a story makes on us is surrender—surrender to the delights of being transported, of encountering experiences, characters, and settings, of considering the truth claims that an author makes by means of his or her story. But we must not be morally and intellectually passive in the face of what an author puts before us. We need to be true to our own convictions as we weigh the morality and truth claims of a story. A story's greatness does not guarantee that it tells the truth in every way.

THE

SCARLET LETTER,

A ROMANCE.

BY

NATHANIEL HAWTHORNE.

BOSTON:
TICKNOR, REED, AND FIELDS.
M DCCC L.

Original title page

The Scarlet Letter: The Book at a Glance

Author. Nathaniel Hawthorne (1804–1864)

Nationality. American

Date of first publication. 1850

Approximate number of pages. 250

Available editions. Probably no work of American literature is more widely available than this work; paperback editions include those by Bantam, Dover Thrift, Norton, Penguin, and Random House.

Genres. Romance novel (with the adjective *romance* here meaning that elements of the supernatural or marvelous are mingled with the prevailing realism of the story); historical fiction

Setting for the story. Boston in Puritan times (mid-seventeenth century)

Main characters. Arthur Dimmesdale, the Puritan minister of the town; Hester Prynne, a married woman with whom Dimmesdale produced an illegitimate daughter named Pearl, also a leading character; Roger Chillingworth, husband of Hester who arrives belatedly in the town and seeks to destroy Dimmesdale as an act of revenge; the Puritan community as a group. No one of these dominates the story more than the others, but inasmuch as Dimmesdale's salvation on the scaffold resolves the action, by the story's end he has emerged as the protagonist.

Story line. The story opens with the public exposure of Hester Prynne, holding an infant daughter whose father she refuses to identify. In punishment, she is ostracized by the Puritan community and forced to wear a scarlet letter A on her bosom. The father of the girl is the town minister, Arthur Dimmesdale, who is too weak-willed to shoulder his share of responsibility for the sin of adultery. Eventually Hester's husband, Roger Chillingworth, arrives in Boston and takes up residence with Dimmesdale. He inflames Dimmesdale's sense of guilt, and Dimmesdale undergoes a long physical and mental decline. In the climax of the story, Dimmesdale, on the verge of death, mounts the scaffold and confesses his sin, experiencing God's forgiveness as he does so.

Five misconceptions about *The Scarlet Letter*. (1) *Hawthorne paints a historically accurate picture of the New England Puritans.* Hawthorne's portrayal of the Puritans is part of his satiric design, and writers of satire exaggerate to make their points. Hawthorne's Puritans have little in common with the original Puritans of Old and New England, and nothing in common with the picture of the Puritans that emerges from their own writings. (2) *The fact that Hawthorne portrays the Puritans negatively demonstrates his rejection of Christianity in this book.* We need to make a distinction between the behavior of the Puritan community and their doctrine. The book ultimately affirms Christian and Puritan *doctrine*, while exposing the *behavior* of the religious community portrayed in the story. (3) *This is a completely gloomy book.* The spectacle of sin and guilt is, indeed, a sad one, but the story moves toward a celebration of Christian salvation, and the characters win other victories along the way. (4) *Hawthorne really did run across a scarlet letter A while working in the local customhouse.* The account that the narrator of *The Scarlet Letter* gives in the preface, entitled "The Custom-House," of finding a scarlet letter is as fictional as the story that follows. Hawthorne never found such a letter. (5) *The story is primarily about adultery.* It isn't. The word *adultery* does not even appear in the book. The adultery is a past event when the story begins. The focus is on the consequences of that past event. No adulterous passions or experiences are portrayed in the book. The story is not about adultery but about concealment of sin and the guilt it produces. It is also about *consciousness* of sin and guilt.

Cultural context. Hawthorne was a mid-nineteenth-century author. The dominant world view in the first half of that century was Romanticism, which elevated nature, feeling, freedom from restraints, and the autonomy of the individual to a position of primacy. Hester represents the Romantic worldview. The Christian worldview existed side by side with the Romantic. The central thematic conflict in *The Scarlet Letter* is the conflict between Romantic and Christian worldviews. We should note in passing that the book adds a third worldview to the mix—Puritan legalism, which elevates law and the moral code to the highest value.

Reception history. *The Scarlet Letter* is probably the signature book of American literature. Certainly no work of American literature is more famous. The book has been a cultural icon from the time of its first publication, when it was an instant best seller.

Tips for reading. (1) Settle down for a leisurely read. Hawthorne covers a relatively small amount of action, but what he does include is described in full detail. (2) Instead of reading for action, therefore, we need to relish characterization, relationships, settings, and interior psychological action (what is happening inside the minds of characters). (3) We need to keep revising our understandings and assessments of characters and worldviews. Through most of the story we would never guess that Dimmesdale and the Christian worldview that he represents would eclipse Hester and Romanticism as the view that Hawthorne endorsed. (4) A lot of what the book expresses about human experience is embodied in symbols.

The Author and His Faith

Nathaniel Hawthorne (1804–1864) was born into a long-established New England family whose names dot the pages of American colonial history. An ancestor had been a judge at the Salem witchcraft trials, and Hawthorne spent a lifetime distancing himself from certain aspects of his Puritan heritage. Hawthorne was not part of the institutional or churchgoing scene in his day. When we speak in this guide of his faith, it is not a comment on his state of soul but on his belief system and (even more) the religious viewpoint embodied in his fiction.

The religious context. Two intellectual/religious systems of belief were candidates for Hawthorne's allegiance. One was Transcendentalism, the American version of Romanticism. Hawthorne dabbled with it (even living briefly at a Transcendental commune called Brook Farm), but he did not share the optimism about human nature that Transcendentalism embraced. So he was left with Christianity as the belief system within which he operated. We can say unequivocally that Hawthorne was a theist with thorough familiarity with the Bible and Christian doctrine.

Hawthorne's religion. Hawthorne's notebooks are filled with references to God, leading a literary critic to say that Hawthorne was "innately religious" and "more than any other writer of his time . . . a God-centered writer" (Joseph Schwartz). His acquaintance with the Bible and reliance on it in his fiction were so thorough that his editor and publisher claimed that when he questioned Hawthorne about his use of a word, Hawthorne would almost always refer him to the Bible as his authority (James T. Fields). Selected Hawthorne scholars claim the following: as a writer Hawthorne was "freely at home in the Hebraic-Christian tradition" (Amos Wilder); Hawthorne's theology was a "nameless and indisputatious" Calvinism or Puritanism, "arrived at by experience and insight" (Austin Warren); Hawthorne is a Protestant writer whose novel *The Scarlet Letter* is the nearest American equivalent to the Catholic novels of the French writer Francois Mauriac (Louis O. Rubin Jr.).

Religion in *The Scarlet Letter*. Any reader of Hawthorne's best-known story can see at a glance that the entire frame of reference is Christian. The religious life of characters in the story revolves around practices like churchgoing, sermons, sin, confession, and catechism. Biblical allusions abound. Christian doctrines such as morality, sin, guilt, heaven, hell, and confession are the assumed frame of reference on virtually every page. It is indisputable that Hawthorne (a) knew Christianity well and (b) incorporated it into his fiction. The degree to which *The Scarlet Letter* moves beyond acquaintance to affirmation will be apparent in the commentary that follows.

CHAPTER 1

The Prison-Door

Plot Summary

The two-page opening chapter whisks us away to an imagined world that on the surface is remote from our own time and place. The story begins with a crowd scene, and the brief description of the men's steeple-crowned hats and the women's hoods is our first clue that we have stepped into seventeenth-century Puritan Boston.

The focus of the chapter is not on the crowd, however, but rather the place where the early action of the story will occur. The crowd has assembled in front of the town prison. The prison is only the launching pad, as the narrator immediately takes a wide-angle view and names the ingredients that made up any typical village in Puritan New England—a church, a surrounding cemetery, and a prison. Then, in a surprise maneuver, Hawthorne gives the most space of all to a wild rosebush beside the prison. It is hard to imagine a simpler introduction to the complex story that will follow.

Commentary

The simple portal through which we enter Hawthorne's masterpiece is a carefully orchestrated introduction to the book as a whole. While seeming merely to describe a physical setting, Hawthorne actually establishes his famous technique of symbolic reality. The prison, the church, the graveyard, and the rosebush are literal properties of the scene, but each one functions as a symbol of an important aspect of Hawthorne's imagined

The opening sentences of any story are one of the biggest challenges facing a storyteller. All storytellers need an irresistible hook that will entice a reader to keep reading. Hawthorne reached into the available bag of tricks and cast his lot with description of place or setting as the thing that would draw his readers into the story.

Whenever we read or listen to a story, we enter a whole world of the imagination. We enter that unfamiliar world much as we enter a real-life place that we are visiting for the first time. Gradually we become familiar with the details and assumptions of the imagined world of the story. A literary critic once remarked that the world of prison, cemetery, and church that we meet at the outset of *The Scarlet Letter* epitomizes the Puritan drama of sin, death, and salvation.

Hawthorne's use of symbolism extends to characters' names. Hester is a version of Esther, an Old Testament heroine noted for her beauty, strength, and courage.

The Scarlet Letter sets the Christian and Romantic worldviews into conflict and lets them fight it out until the end of the story. The Romantic worldview elevates feeling and nature to the highest value and disparages human civilization or society as being confining to the human spirit. It is part of Hawthorne's technique of the guilty reader initially to get us to feel sympathetically toward the Romantic elevation of nature and feeling.

Despite the opening portrayal of society as rigid and nature as warm and sympathetic, it is important not to foreclose on which worldview Hawthorne ultimately favors. *The Scarlet Letter* is built around a surprise ending that reverses our opening impressions.

world. The prison symbolizes the evil that is part of human nature and society. The church represents salvation as Christians experience it. The cemetery symbolizes death, and the rosebush embodies the principle of nature and natural feeling or emotion.

While the technique of symbolic reality is something that any careful reader can see by looking closely at the text, another technique is one that we do not fully realize until the end of the story. It is the technique of the guilty reader. Hawthorne uses evaluative terms that on a first reading evoke a negative picture of society and Puritanism and a positive picture of natural sentiment (as symbolized by the rosebush). This might mislead us into thinking that the book is an attack on Christianity. But as the story unfolds it becomes clear that the book itself accepts evil and its punishment as inevitable aspects of human existence, not something foisted on it by Christianity.

For Reflection or Discussion

A good preliminary question to ask of any episode in a story is, What draws me into the action? What evokes my interest? Secondly, Hawthorne uses heavily evaluative terms as he describes the details that he puts before us, and these function as a lens through which we look at such phenomena as the prison and the rosebush. This prompts us to ask, How does Hawthorne initially get us to view such dichotomies as civilization and nature, society and the individual, Christianity and Romanticisim? What specific things characterize the two halves of these dichotomies?

CHAPTER 2
The Market-Place

Plot Summary

A crowd of spectators stands outside the prison in the town of Boston. Townspeople are speaking condemningly about a notorious adulteress in their midst. In a moment of high drama, the prison door is flung open and a young woman steps into the sunlight. Her name is Hester Prynne. She is an unmarried mother and carries an infant in her arms. A red letter A is embroidered on the front of her blouse, symbolizing adultery. After Hester steps into public gaze, the onlookers continue to utter a stream of judgmental condemnation of Hester as they talk among themselves.

Commentary

As this chapter unfolds in the same leisurely pace that characterized the opening chapter, it becomes apparent that Hawthorne has no interest whatever in a fast-paced narrative style that keeps us on the edge of our seats with an abundance of external action. Hawthorne has not written an "action story" that makes us wonder what happens next. Instead he has written a story that casts the focus on two other things—the description of people and settings and the interior action of what happens inside people's minds and hearts.

The key to interpreting this chapter is to view it as an expansion of the conflict that was latent in the first chapter. Hester is the engaging and sympathetic figure as she endures the shame of her punishment as a victim of social prejudice. She represents nineteenth-century Romanticism, in the

In this chapter Hawthorne reenacts what Romantic literature of his era repeatedly portrayed. It is the spectacle of the solitary person victimized by a hostile society.

Hawthorne labeled the kind of stories that he wrote "romances," and this means that they are not novels. Novels are realistic and lifelike in their surface details. Romances move beyond the strictly realistic. The extreme idealization of Hester and satiric portrayal of the Puritans illustrate this. The technique is that of caricature, not realism. No woman is as perfect as Hester is portrayed as being, and probably no society has ever been as single-mindedly judgmental as the Puritans of Hawthorne's story.

World making is one of Hawthorne's greatest gifts. Instead of reading to catch the plotline, we need to relish Hawthorne's ability to describe scenes and people.

A literary critic described Henry James's technique of the guilty reader this way: "James managed to seduce all but the most attentive readers into identifying initially with a point of view which seems sensible and . . . sympathetic. It is only with the unfolding of the action that we . . . come to understand that the original point of view was stupid, unimaginative, shabby, and evil."
—Joseph Summers, *The Muse's Method*

Hawthorne plants the seeds of his eventual exposure of Hester already in this chapter. Having compared Hester to the Madonna (Mary and Jesus), the narrator notes unobtrusively that here, in contrast to Mary, "there was the taint of deepest sin in the most sacred quality of human life." He also calls the scene that is unfolding in this chapter "the spectacle of guilt and shame in a fellow-creature" (that is, Hester). The narrator is our ally against the difficulties of reading Hawthorne's story, in this case giving us hints that Hester is not a completely sympathetic figure.

specific form of the ostracized individual set over against a hostile society. Storytelling is an affective art in which the storyteller gets us to feel a certain way toward characters and actions. Initially *The Scarlet Letter* gets us to feel sympathetically toward Hester as Romantic heroine.

Set over against Hester is the Puritan community. They are "a people amongst whom religion and law were almost identical." We need to keep the issues clear at this point. The Puritan community does not represent Christianity. Puritan behavior as portrayed in Hawthorne's story is less than Christian, knowing nothing of the spirit of Galatians 6:1–2: "Brothers, if anyone is caught in any transgression, you who are spiritual should restore him in a spirit of gentleness. . . . Bear one another's burdens, and so fulfill the law of Christ." As the story unfolds, we will see with increasing clarity the wedge that Hawthorne drives between Puritan behavior and Christian doctrine. In the early stages of the book, only two worldviews are evident—the Romantic, which elevates feeling, and the Puritan, which makes law the central fact of life. We need to keep reading before the Christian worldview gradually emerges.

Of course the technique of symbolism is alive and well in the second chapter. Images of light and darkness, of rigidity like iron and seasoned wood, and of solitary suffering versus societal judgmentalism pervade the pages of this chapter.

For Reflection or Discussion

The focus of interpretive attention for this chapter needs to be on characterization. Hester is the sympathetic central character in this chapter, so the first thing to do is go through the chapter and compile a portrait of Hester. By what techniques and evaluative vocabulary does the storyteller get us to sympathize with Hester? Additionally, what things make Hester a Romantic heroine in the nineteenth-century sense of that word? Secondarily, we need to compile a portrait of the Puritan community. What is the essential identity of the Puritans? Specifically, how do they represent a legalistic worldview that elevates law to the highest value? Having done justice to characterization, we should note the patterns of imagery and symbolism by which Hawthorne presents the solitary sufferer and the tormenting community in which she lives.

Literature is the voice of authentic human experience. In this chapter Hawthorne paints a moving picture of suffering humanity and the individual's rejection by a self-righteous society. The picture of social prejudice in Hawthorne's story is as up-to-date as the daily news.

CHAPTER 3

The Recognition

Plot Summary

Hawthorne structured the opening chapters of his book on a progressive principle in which readers are introduced to various characters in a carefully orchestrated sequence. The opening chapter described the village where the main action will occur. The second chapter introduced two mighty antagonists—Hester and the Puritan society. Chapter 3 now adds two more leading characters.

We are first introduced to someone whose name we learn in a later chapter. He is Roger Chillingworth, the husband of Hester who was delayed in joining his wife in the new world. The other person who is added to the cast of characters in this chapter is Rev. Arthur Dimmesdale, the local minister and father of Hester Prynne's daughter.

Roger Chillingworth and Arthur Dimmesdale are introduced to us in the same chapter. That is no coincidence. Although Dimmesdale does not know it until late in the action, Chillingworth becomes his archenemy—a demonic figure who tries to destroy Dimmesdale's soul. Their names are symbolic. Chillingworth combines the suggestions of coldheartedness with a once-worthy aspect of character. Arthur evokes the idealized associations of the Arthurian legend, but Dimmesdale—"dim as a dale"—highlights both evil and concealment of truth.

Storytellers can scarcely ply their trade without resorting to dramatic irony, but *The Scarlet Letter* is unsurpassed in the technique. Dramatic irony arises when readers know more than what some of the characters in the story know. The concealment of Dimmesdale's status as Hester's partner in adultery is the main source of irony in *The Scarlet Letter*, but other notable instances are present as well.

We do not learn a lot about either character in this chapter, but they are now on our radar screen as actors in the central drama.

The main action of chapter 3 is Hester's refusal to name the father of her child. That refusal is made in the face of tremendous attempts to force disclosure of the father's name. The first attempt at coercion is made by Rev. John Wilson. That is followed by Rev. Dimmesdale's appeal to Hester in an emotion-packed scene.

Commentary

The Scarlet Letter starts out simply and then becomes progressively more complicated and subtle. Chapter 3 makes greater demands on us than the first two chapters did.

The deeper meanings of this chapter are embodied in the dramatic irony that Hawthorne decided to highlight. This irony starts with the opening conversation between a townsman and Roger Chillingworth, husband of Hester. The townsman offers the opinion that Chillingworth must be glad to see justice so rigorously enforced in the town at which he has arrived, and Chillingworth inquires, seemingly innocuously, whether the father of Hester's child is known. As readers we sense, as the townsman does not, the hidden significance of Chillingworth's question.

But that is only a warm-up to the irony that swirls about Rev. Dimmesdale. Rev. Wilson prevails on Dimmesdale to implore Hester to reveal the father's name because as Hester's pastor he knows her "natural temper better than I." When Dimmesdale appeals to Hester, he asks in a question dripping with irony, "What can thy silence do for him [the father of the child], except it tempt him—yea, compel him, as it were—to add hypocrisy to sin?" Of course the spectators do not sense the significance of that statement, but it is in fact the main plotline of the story that follows. Equally ironic is Dimmesdale's parting shot, "Wondrous strength and generosity of a woman's heart! She will not speak!"

But the greatest irony lies at a deeper level. On the surface, Hester has acted heroically in not implicating her partner in adultery. She is all heart. She wishes she "could endure his agony, as well as mine." On a first reading, we are inclined to think, "How noble." What irony, therefore, when we stop to consider that we have witnessed a moral crime in Hester's apparent selflessness, as she herself will later admit to Dimmesdale.

As always in this story, we must distinguish between Puritan behavior and Christian doctrine. There are numerous hints of the Christian worldview in this chapter, even though it has not fully emerged as a combatant to Hester's Romantic worldview. Chillingworth, for example, offers the opinion that the guilty father might stand silently, "forgetting that God sees him." The narrator calls Hester's infant "a sin-born infant in her arms." Hester's heart is said to be "an erring woman's heart," entangled by a "mesh of good and evil."

For Reflection or Discussion

As already intimated, Hawthorne raises the bar of difficulty with this chapter. The first thing to trace is the continuation and amplification of Hester's Romantic outlook, with its elevation of feeling as the highest value. As an extension of that, we need to note how Hawthorne gives us repeated opportunities to be guilty readers, sympathizing with

Hawthorne continues to use the technique of caricature in his portrayal of the Puritan community in this chapter. Rev. Wilson is so accustomed to the darkness of his study that he blinks as he stands in the sunlight, with his "grizzled locks beneath his skull-cap." Governor Bellingham is of course dressed in black. And so forth.

Hawthorne's love of symbolism largely recedes in this chapter, with one notable exception. After Hester refuses to disclose who the infant's father is, Dimmesdale emits a long sigh "with his hand upon his heart." This is the first instance of a symbolic gesture that will come to dominate the middle of the story. The pain in Dimmesdale's heart is a symbol of his guilty conscience and soul.

Hester in ways that the book will eventually condemn. Additionally, we need to explore the dramatic irony that pervades the chapter, along the lines suggested above. This irony is not present just for the narrative voltage that it supplies, though we need to be receptive of that voltage. The irony functions as part of the battle between Romantic and Christian worldviews that will eventually be fully established. Finally, what signposts begin to establish the Christian worldview as an alternative to Hester's Romantic elevation of feeling as the thing that should determine human behavior?

CHAPTER 4

The Interview

Plot Summary

The title of the chapter identifies the main action. With Hester having returned to her prison cell, she is visited by her husband, a doctor who has been given the task of giving Hester a medical checkup after the trauma of the day. The action unfolds in three stages. First Chillingworth attends to Hester's physical needs as any conscientious doctor would. Then a section of dialogue fills in the details of the ill-advised marriage between Chillingworth and Hester, temperamental opposites who should never have married. The third and crucial action comes at the end of the chapter as Chillingworth vows revenge on Hester's partner in adultery.

It is a principle of storytelling that we need a back-and-forth rhythm between intensity and relaxation of tension. After the extreme intensity of the previous chapter, where Hester resisted pressure to disclose the father's name, this chapter allows us to catch our breath.

Commentary

A good avenue toward interpretation of this chapter is to ask about its function in the ongoing story. The answer is that it fills in important pieces of information for the larger story. Once Hawthorne decided to make Hester's husband a personal antagonist for Dimmesdale, we are naturally curious about the nature of the marriage and how it relates to Hester's adultery. The interview between Hester and Chillingworth tells us what we need to know.

Secondly, the revenge motif is the third most important ingredient in the plot, behind the story of Dimmesdale's guilt-induced physical and emotional decline and Hester's fluctuating fortunes. We can scarcely avoid shuddering in the concluding paragraphs of the chapter as we listen to Chillingworth vow revenge on his as yet unknown personal enemy.

For Reflection or Discussion

Hawthorne puts on the agenda of our attention the question of what kind of marriage Chillingworth and Hester had; what does he want us to understand about that marriage? Second, at the end of the chapter Chillingworth makes predictions regarding what he will do to Hester's partner in adultery; what are the key predictions?

Revenge has been a leading motif through the annals of storytelling, probably because it is an impulse that lies deep in the human heart. While some narrative traditions have valorized revenge, it is to Hawthorne's credit that he makes us feel both the horror and ignominy of pursuing revenge against a fellow human, as embodied in Chillingworth's pursuit of a vendetta against Dimmesdale.

As Chillingworth vows revenge at the end of the chapter, he foreshadows much of the rest of the story. In addition to the revenge that will determine much of the ensuing action, Chillingworth highlights the fact that only he will know what is happening. In other words, dramatic irony will pervade the story.

CHAPTER 5

Hester at Her Needle

Plot Summary

The chapter title signals that this chapter will be devoted to the development of Hester's characterization, especially as it relates to her social standing in the community. As Hester forges a life at the end of her confinement in prison, she emerges as an example of courage and fortitude. Refusing to flee from the town that has rejected her, she makes a living and wins a degree of acceptance in the community on the strength of her skill in sewing and embroidery. Hester is also a model of charity. None of this eliminates her status as an outsider, and a result of her ostracism as an adulteress is that she has "a sympathetic knowledge of the hidden sin in other hearts."

Commentary

The experience that Hawthorne portrays in this chapter is redemptive suffering—the virtues that can be engendered in a person who undergoes suffering. A good avenue toward organizing the chapter is to trace two primary threads and observe how the flow of narrative swings back and forth between them.

One thread is Hester's suffering as the solitary and ostracized sinner. Hawthorne systematically delineates the dimensions of Hester's isolation in her community. A subordinate aspect of this is the continuing satiric exposure of Puritan rigidity, but that is no more than a backdrop to the idealization of Hester. Hawthorne rings the changes on how completely solitary Hester's existence is in a community that rejects her as a sinner. The cumulative impact of these glimpses is to generate tremendous sympathy for Hester as a victimized individual.

In addition to the ongoing picture of suffering, Hawthorne paints a picture of Hester winning a degree of acceptance by strength of character and good deeds. The chapter is thus a balance between negative and positive features of Hester's life in the community. The positive theme consists of the

All literary narratives are built on a principle of rhythm—a back-and-forth flow between two motifs that a give part of the story features. This chapter flows back and forth between the suffering of Hester as an ostracized sinner and a humanistic redemption on a social level that she wins by her exemplary conduct in the community.

In this chapter Hawthorne does not "flag" his design of making Hester a Romantic heroine in the nineteenth-century sense of that word. But as readers we need to keep that design in view. The solitary protagonist is a leading archetype of Romantic literature, and Hester is such a figure in this chapter.

place that Hester wins for herself as a result of her abilities and moral fiber.

An additional piece in Hawthorne's design is the latent tension between Christian and Romantic. Hester fits the pattern of the isolated Romantic protagonist perfectly. But Hawthorne uses Christian terminology to describe the Romanticism that Hester embodies. For example, as Hester debates within herself whether to flee or stay, she decides that here "had been the scene of her guilt" where she could, by enduring suffering, "at length purge her soul" and achieve a "saint-like" purity that would be "the result of martyrdom." Again, she came to view her sewing and embroidery as a "penance" and "sacrifice."

We need to interpret carefully here. On the one hand, the Christian terminology lends an aura of approval to Hester. But in view of the eventual open conflict between Romanticism and Christianity that will emerge as the story unfolds, we need to store away these signposts that the Christian worldview is also operative in the story. The Romantic values embodied by Hester in this chapter are sometimes couched in Christian terms, but that does not make Hester an exemplar of Christianity.

For Reflection or Discussion

The right questions to pursue have been implied in the foregoing commentary. In what ways does the text idealize Hester? In what ways are we made to sympathize with her? Where are we made aware that Hawthorne intends his portrait to be that of a Romantic heroine, and what are the latent signs that this Romanticism is in tension with a Christian worldview?

The subject of literature is universal human experience. The particulars of literature, C. S. Lewis claimed, are a net whereby the author expresses the universal. Hawthorne is a master at capturing universal human experience. In this chapter we are led to feel the reality of isolation, loneliness, victimization, prejudice, recognition of hidden sin in people, and redemptive suffering.

The juxtaposition of Romantic sentiment and Christian worldview is highlighted in a single sentence: "She was patient—a martyr, indeed—but she forbore to pray for her enemies." *She forbore to pray for her enemies*: that explodes with meaning for any Christian reader. Jesus commanded people to pray for their enemies and did so himself as he hung from the cross.

CHAPTER 6
Pearl

Plot Summary

There is a sense in which Hester's infant daughter has been in the cast of characters from the beginning, but we have never been formally introduced to her. Hawthorne makes that introduction in this chapter. The characterization of Pearl is the main narrative business of chapter 6. The large amount of attention that Hawthorne allots to Pearl shows that she is important to his purposes. Upon analysis, that importance consists of Pearl's contribution to the larger patterns of the story, inasmuch as she herself does not play a major role in the action. To relish this chapter, a reader needs to settle down to a "fireside chat" with the author as he talks about a character in leisurely descriptive manner.

Pearl fills four main roles in the story: (1) she symbolizes the adultery that is the mainspring of the action; (2) she is the victim of her parents' adultery, thus embodying the principle of consequences for sin; (3) she is an agent of retribution to her parents, making it impossible for them to ignore their sin; (4) she is the object of Puritan bigotry and sadism.

Hawthorne placed a crucial piece of foreshadowing in the first paragraph of this chapter when he says that Pearl was destined "to be finally a blessed soul in heaven." We will not know until the final confession scene how that prediction can be true.

Commentary

Hawthorne chose not to use realism as his mode in portraying Pearl. He accentuates her symbolic meanings, for example. Her name itself is a symbol and allusion. Jesus told a parable about a pearl of great price, and Hester's naming her Pearl hints at both the value that Hester feels toward her offspring and the bitterness that Hester feels regarding what the birth of a daughter has cost her in social standing. The imagery that Hawthorne attaches to Pearl contributes to the effect of fantasy and symbolism in place of realism, with the vocabulary of *spirit*, *elf*, and *dryad* consistently applied to her. A summary statement is that Hester "could not help questioning . . . whether Pearl was a human child."

One unifying element in the characterization

of Pearl in this chapter is that she is an extension of her mother's character and social situation. Pearl lives beyond the pale of human society. She is the product of passion and a broken law. She is dominated by impulse. She is strongly associated with nature. An overall ambivalence governs her characterization, as sometimes she is idealized and other times even called "a demon offspring." Pearl is as much a representative of Romanticism as her mother, and her kinship with nature is an important part of that identity.

The most significant aspect of the characterization of Pearl in this chapter is the ambivalence with which we experience her. She is as much a Romantic person as her mother—solitary, living beyond the human community, a figure of nature, defiant, impulsive, filled with vitality. From a Romantic viewpoint, these qualities make Pearl attractive, but Hawthorne fills the chapter with a contrary assessment of her.

For Reflection or Discussion

The key to understanding and relishing this lengthy portrait of Pearl is to trace the ambivalence of the portrait. What aspects idealize Pearl? Where are we made to feel critical of her?

Hawthorne continues to plant seeds that establish an undercurrent of Christian sentiment in the prevailingly positive portrayal of Hester's Romanticism. One of them is the passing comment that Hester "knew that her deed had been evil; she could have no faith, therefore, that its result [Pearl] would be for good."

"It has been said that in *The Scarlet Letter* Hawthorne made a study of three types of sin—'the revealed sin of Hester, the concealed sin of Dimmesdale, and the unpardonable sin of Chillingworth.' But he also dealt with a fourth type—the inherited sin of Pearl."—Barbara Garlitz, "Pearl: 1850–1955"

CHAPTER 7

The Governor's Hall

Plot Summary

After two chapters devoted to characterization, the story swings back to a focus on plot. It is true that this chapter functions mainly to set the stage for a major confrontation that will occur in the next chapter. But with the mention of an organized movement among civil and religious leaders in the community to deprive Hester of her daughter, our instinct for plot conflict is fully aroused. Of course storytellers are fond of delaying an impending event as a way of generating anticipation, and that is what Hawthorne does in this chapter. He meanders through further characterization of Pearl and extensive descriptions of the governor's mansion where the meeting will occur.

The encounter that is foreshadowed in this chapter is vintage Romanticism: the lone individual confronting a hostile society. In this chapter Hawthorne allows Christianity to recede from view and throws the entire light on Puritan behavior, which is portrayed unsympathetically.

Commentary

Hawthorne's technique of creating a world of symbolic reality returns with this chapter. Even more than in the previous chapter devoted to Pearl, the small girl emerges as the very embodiment of the Romantic spirit. Additionally, as the product of her mother's adultery, Pearl is directly said to be "the scarlet letter endowed with life."

Even more emphatically, the governor's house emerges as a set piece of symbolic description. Houses in stories are an extension of personality, and Hawthorne makes the governor's hall (the title of the chapter, we need to remember) an expanding picture of Puritan rigidity and lack of feeling. In fact, Hawthorne is so relentless in the negative image patterns that he associates with the hall that we can say that the technique of satiric caricature has returned to the story.

Hawthorne's portrait of Puritan society is governed by the dynamics of literary satire (the exposure of human vice). Exaggeration is a common feature of satire. Probably no group in the history of the world has been as single-mindedly rigid and uncaring as Hawthorne's fictional Puritans.

A key symbolic moment occurs at the very end of the chapter. Pearl sees a rosebush and clamors for a red rose. The rose is symbolic of nature and feeling, here established as a foil to all of the Puritan rigidity that has dominated the chapter.

For Reflection or Discussion

How does Hawthorne manage the ongoing description of Pearl in such a way as to reinforce her as an embodiment of the Romantic spirit? What descriptive details perpetuate the characterization of the

Puritan community established early in the book, and in particular their rigidity and lack of feeling?

CHAPTER 8

The Elf-Child and the Minister

Plot Summary

The anticipated encounter between Hester and the civil and religious establishment occupies this chapter. It is the most intense scene since the attempt to force Hester to disclose the identity of her partner in adultery. The overall action is the moment of decision that will determine whether Hester will be allowed to retain custody of Pearl. The sequence of the chapter unfolds in three segments. First, Governor Bellingham interacts with the impish Pearl. Then Hester makes her appeal to be allowed to retain the care of her child. Finally Dimmesdale's counsel that Hester be allowed to keep her child is accepted by his colleagues.

Commentary

The plot summary of the chapter barely hints at the fireworks that are actually exploding as the action unfolds. We can trust the titles that storytellers give us to provide helpful interpretive frameworks, and the mention of the elf-child in this chapter's title gives us the blueprint for the first half of the chapter. Pearl's identity as a Romantic child of nature is strongly developed here, climaxing in the child's assertion that she had not been born by human means "but had been plucked by her mother off the bush of wild roses, that grew by the prison-door."

Biblical allusions pack a big punch in this chapter. For example, Rev. Wilson tells Pearl that she must heed Christian instruction so that she may wear in her bosom "the pearl of great price." Hester tells Dimmesdale, "Thou knowest me better than these men can," with the verb *know* being the biblical word for sexual union. Dimmesdale proposes that the men "fast and pray" on the question of the father's identity.

Hawthorne is a master of irony. We know, while Dimmesdale's colleagues do not, what the import is when Dimmesdale says that "the sinful mother [is] happier than the sinful father" for having her sin revealed. We know what is happening, but other characters do not, when Roger Chillingworth responds to Dimmesdale's statement with the comment, "You speak, my friend, with a strange earnestness."

Symbolic gestures embody much of the deeper meanings of this chapter—Pearl's claim to have been plucked off a rosebush, Dimmesdale's hand over his heart, his "careworn and emaciated" physical appearance, the domestic moment of child and father kissing each other.

Hawthorne structured his story as two pyramids. In the first half of the book, the mood gradually rises as Hester triumphs over social prejudice, climaxing in chapter 8 as Hester is allowed to retain custody of Pearl. We will descend from this high point as we trace the decline of Dimmesdale.

The second half of the equation announced in the chapter title is "and the minister." Dimmesdale had dropped from sight after his brief appeal to Hester in the opening scene of the book to reveal the father's identity. Hawthorne is about to make him a leading character in the story (and eventually the protagonist). The most intense moment in the chapter—and a moment dripping with dramatic irony—comes when Hester appeals to Dimmesdale to take up her cause, with the statement, "Thou wast my pastor, and hadst charge of my soul, and knowest me better than these men can." Dimmesdale responds with a symbolic gesture that will come to dominate the story when he holds "his hand over his heart," symbolic of his guilty conscience. The two halves of the chapter title come together in the final pages of the chapter when Pearl goes to Dimmesdale, takes his hand, and kisses it, which is followed by Dimmesdale's kissing Pearl on her brow. It is a classic moment in the story.

The apparent plot of the story thus far has been the triumph of the Romantic world view over our sympathies; the hidden plot has been the counter presence of the Christian worldview. The latter exerts itself strongly in this chapter. For example, Hester utters such sentiments as that "God gave me the child," and that Pearl is endowed with "the power of retribution for my sin." Most important of all, Dimmesdale advises the assembled authorities, "Better to fast and pray upon it; and still better, it may be, to leave the mystery as we find it, unless Providence reveal it of its own accord." That is exactly what will happen at the story's climax.

For Reflection or Discussion

One pattern to trace is the obvious Romanticism of the chapter. How is Pearl an embodiment of the Romantic spirit? How does Hawthorne handle Pearl's Romantic spirit in an ambivalent way (both sympathetic and unsympathetic)? How does Hester's standing up for her rights fit into a Romantic viewpoint? The second focus of the chapter is Dimmesdale, and here we need to look for answers to the question of how Hawthorne plants seeds of foreshadowing in the actions of Dimmesdale in the late stages of the chapter.

CHAPTER 9

The Leech

Plot Summary

The title of the chapter seems to promise that the focus will be the characterization of Chillingworth, but that is not what actually happens. A main component of the unfolding plot of the story is the interaction between Chillingworth and Dimmesdale, and this chapter narrates how they came to live together. As this relationship and living arrangement are explained, two further plot motifs heat up—Dimmesdale's guilt-induced physical decline and Chillingworth's obsession with exacting revenge.

The first piece of irony is the chapter title. Leech was an old term for "doctor," based on the practice of using leeches to suck blood and therefore bring health. Chillingworth is literally like a leech, drawing the vitality from Dimmesdale, unbeknown to anyone except Chillingworth.

Commentary

Two techniques claim our attention in this chapter. One is dramatic irony, which will now dominate the middle chapters of *The Scarlet Letter*. As readers, we know what Dimmesdale and the

Chillingworth belongs to a long literary lineage that has portrayed self-destructive evil. Like Milton's Satan, Chillingworth builds his whole life around the destruction of someone else, only to destroy himself.

The revenge motif has been important in the history of literature and theology. The impulse to "get even" lies deep in the human psyche, which probably explains why it has been such a prominent subject for stories and plays through the centuries. In Christian theology, the desire for personal revenge has always been condemned, which probably explains why Hawthorne draws a link between Chillingworth and Satan near the end of the chapter.

Storytellers love to employ foils—two characters or actions in which one sets off the other, usually by being a contrast but sometimes by being a parallel. In Hawthorne's story, the declines of Dimmesdale and Chillingworth are parallel rails on the same train track.

townspeople do not, namely, that Chillingworth is his personal enemy bent on exacting revenge for Dimmesdale's sexual union with his wife. We cringe in an awareness that Chillingworth will manipulate Dimmesdale's psychic and physical decline in his role as physician. Chillingworth is the last person in the world who should move in as Dimmesdale's housemate. Virtually everything that Chillingworth initiates—walks on the seashore or in the forest, long conversations, hanging the wall with a tapestry of the story of David and Bathsheba—possesses voltage for us as insiders on what is really happening.

The second technique that is highlighted is symbolic reality, with numerous details being both literal and embodiments of hidden realities. Dimmesdale's gesture of placing his hand over his heart, accompanied by an obvious physical decline, exemplifies psychosomatic illness brought on by a guilty conscience and the stress that a cover-up brings. But Chillingworth also undergoes a transformation as a result in his role as revenger. There is now "something ugly and evil in his face, which [others] had not previously noticed."

For Reflection or Discussion

What are the evidences of irony in this chapter? What literary effects do they produce in a reader? Where does symbolism figure prominently?

CHAPTER 10

The Leech and His Patient

Plot Summary

Hawthorne knew that he had a good thing going with the ironic relationship between Dimmesdale and Chillingworth, so he devoted a second chapter to the matter. The previous chapter set up the narrative situation, and this chapter further develops the relationship, chiefly by means of drama or dialogue, with interspersed narration by the storyteller. As we listen to specimen conversations between Chillingworth and Dimmesdale, we accompany Chillingworth on his voyage of discovery and revenge.

The climax of the chapter moves beyond realism to fantasy, in confirmation of Hawthorne's claim that he wrote romances, in which inclusion of the supernatural is always part of the story. As Dimmesdale is entranced in a deep sleep, Chillingworth places his hand on the minister's heart. We are not told exactly what Chillingworth discerned, but we infer that it is the secret of Dimmesdale's guilty relationship with Hester. Hawthorne throws the emphasis on Chillingworth's ecstatic response, comparing it to Satan's glee when he gains a human soul for his demonic kingdom.

Commentary

The significance of what is happening in this chapter will emerge if we grasp the narrative conventions that dominate the action. The first of these is the detective story. In a detective story, the detective gathers data and sifts through it, gradually groping his way toward discovery of who com-

As with chapter 9, the chapter title springs the first instance of irony on us. There is irony in Hawthorne's using the old term for "doctor"—leech—inasmuch as Chillingworth extracts not only the truth from Dimmesdale but also his health. But it is even more ironic to name Dimmesdale's external role of patient; he is really the sworn personal foe of Chillingworth.

The enjoyment of this chapter hinges on our relishing the sparring that goes on between Chillingworth and Dimmesdale. To cite just one example, Chillingworth remarks that "many a poor soul hath given its confidence to me," and "what a relief have I witnessed in those sinful brethren." Dimmesdale counters by saying that some men keep "silent by the very constitution of their nature" or by "a zeal for God's glory and man's welfare." The whole chapter is permeated by such exchanges.

Like Samuel Taylor Coleridge in his story "The Rime of the Ancient Mariner," Hawthorne tells two stories at the same time. The strategy is highlighted in this chapter. At one level, Dimmesdale's decline is a psychological experience; today we would call it a case of psychosomatic illness—a physical ailment brought on by psychological causes. But Hawthorne tells a moral and spiritual story as well as a psychological one. This plotline is a story of guilt.

Christian references thrust themselves to the surface at several key points in this chapter. One is the moment at which Chillingworth presses Dimmesdale to confess his sin to him. Dimmesdale blurts out, "If it be the soul's disease, then do I commit myself to the one Physician of the soul! . . . Who art thou . . . that dares thrust himself between the sufferer and his God?"

mitted the crime. In turn, the criminal tries to avoid detection. That this is part of Hawthorne's intention is evident from the statement early in the chapter that Chillingworth "had begun an investigation" with the "integrity of a judge, desirous only of the truth." Shortly thereafter we hear Chillingworth say, "Let us dig a little farther in the direction of this vein." And then there is the ecstatic conclusion of the chapter, which resembles a group of detectives giving each other "high fives" the moment they solve a crime.

Other statements in the chapter make it more than a simple detective story. Chillingworth asks so many leading questions that we begin to wonder if perhaps he already knows the truth and is simply manipulating and tormenting a victim in pursuit of revenge. At such points the story is what is familiarly called a "cat and mouse" story in which a person simply plays with a victim for the enjoyment of tormenting him. This is especially the case when, in response to hearing the laughter of Pearl, Chillingworth starts to ask Dimmesdale questions about Hester, and whether Hester is less miserable than the unknown father for having her crime revealed rather than concealed.

Of course Hawthorne is a born symbolist, and he indulges that interest here as well. Digging into Dimmesdale's heart is like digging into a grave. "A bodily disease," says Chillingworth, "may, after all, be but a symptom of some ailment in the spiritual part." "A strange sympathy betwixt soul and body!" exclaims Chillingworth.

Finally, for all the symbolism in this chapter, it is also filled with the realism of life as we know it. There is realism when Chillingworth pushes Dimmesdale too far and asks him to confess, whereupon Dimmesdale rushes out of the room. Likewise with the psychosomatic affliction of Dimmesdale: it is hard to believe that Hawthorne, with his familiarity with the Bible, did not model his story on David's experience as recorded in Psalm 32:3–4: "When I kept silence, my bones waxed old through my roaring all the day long. For day and night thy hand was heavy upon me: my moisture is turned into the drought of summer" (KJV).

For Reflection or Discussion
What things make this chapter a detective story par excellence? If you are familiar with Shakespeare's play *Hamlet*, what parallels do you see between Chillingworth's pursuit of Dimmesdale and Hamlet's sifting of Claudius during the first half of the play? What biblical examples of the guilt-haunted sinner come to mind, and how do they form a subtext for your experience of this chapter?

CHAPTER 11
The Interior of a Heart

Plot Summary
The chapter title says it all: this chapter will be devoted to a portrayal of interior action. The story line revolves around human psychology, and in particular the psychology of guilt. Once we grant that premise, it is as exciting as any story of external action.

The first three paragraphs make it seem as though this chapter will be a continuation of the previous one. They introduce Chillingworth into

In this chapter Hawthorne embodies variations on the theme of the opening verses of Psalm 32, with the starting premise, "When I kept silence." In *The Scarlet Letter*, as in the psalm, there is no relief from guilt without confession. If the sin is public, the confession must be public. That is Dimmesdale's problem, as it was King David's problem.

Some chapters in *The Scarlet Letter* narrate external action. The action in this chapter is inner and spiritual, and it is accordingly one of the subtlest chapters in the book. In particular, Hawthorne portrays the ways in which Dimmesdale does actually confess to being a sinner but in such a way as to make him seem even more saintly in the eyes of his congregation.

the picture and repeat the emphasis of chapter 10 on the doctor's manipulation of Dimmesdale into a state of heightened guilt and corresponding physical decline. A summary statement is that "the victim was for ever on the rack."

But after this preliminary action Chillingworth is dismissed. The person who undertakes an exploration of the minister's psyche is not Chillingworth but the narrator of the story. He is the one we accompany on a journey of spiritual and psychological discovery. This is one chapter among others that justify the claim that Hawthorne gave American literature its classic study of the psychology of guilt.

Commentary

Hawthorne is not content with portraying generalized guilt. He gives us a specific form of guilt. It is highly relevant to the action that Dimmesdale is a Christian minister. He is in the public eye and is considered by his parishioners to be a paragon of spiritual piety and moral virtue. This public role, in turn, determines the form that his struggle with guilt takes.

With that framework in place, we can see how Hawthorne composed a fourfold sequence in this chapter. First the narrator places Dimmesdale into a circle of the spiritual "best of the best" by temperament—a minister who without his burden of guilt would have climbed the "high mount-peaks of faith and sanctity." But his burden of crime and anguish "kept him down, on a level with the lowest." This is the first dimension of Dimmesdale's guilt—a spiritual tragedy in which a single flaw drags the victim down from spiritual attainment.

Second, and ironically, this very burden of

guilt "gave him sympathies so intimate with the sinful brotherhood of mankind." Equipped with this bond of sympathy, the minister becomes all the more elevated in people's spiritual estimate of him. The members of his church "deemed the young clergyman a miracle of holiness." This is the second dimension of his guilt—the growing chasm between Dimmesdale's consciousness of sin and his valorization by his congregation.

Third, there is the suffering brought on by what Dimmesdale himself calls his status as "remorseful hypocrite." He is aware of the hypocrisy of his situation—deemed a member of the spiritually elite when he is actually guilty of the twin sins of adultery and cowardice. By this point in the story Dimmesdale's adultery has receded into the background. The foreground action is now his hypocrisy.

Finally, in a move that it is hard to know how to interpret, Hawthorne pictures Dimmesdale as engaging in Roman Catholic practices of self-laceration. He beats himself with a scourge. He keeps nighttime vigils. He fasts. He stares at himself in a mirror by lamplight. He has hallucinations of accusing acquaintances pointing their fingers at him.

We cannot remind ourselves too often that this story is as much about *the consciousness of sin and guilt* as it is about the sin of adultery itself. It is a story about the consequences of sin (spiritual and psychological) more than about the sin that started the drama that unfolds before us.

For Reflection or Discussion

If we begin with the premise that Hawthorne was a master in the portrayal of the psychology

There are more than twenty images naming colors in this chapter. All but two of them are images of darkness and light, black and white. The general import of this is that Dimmesdale's heart is a battleground between evil and good, falsehood and truth.

In the middle of the chapter Hawthorne enlists an archetype of Christian literature when he portrays Dimmesdale's guilt as a burden that weighs him down. The burden of sin that must be loosed reverberates through Christian literature. The most famous example occurs in John Bunyan's *The Pilgrim's Progress*, in which Christian leaves the City of Destruction with a burden of sin on his back, losing it at the foot of the cross.

of guilt, we can look for answers to the question of how he managed to achieve such impact in his portrayal. Secondly, in what ways can we see real-life experience in Dimmesdale's sad career as a guilt-haunted sinner? Additionally, we can reflect on the vulnerable state of public models of virtue, such as ministers.

CHAPTER 12

The Minister's Vigil

Plot Summary

Hawthorne carefully structured his story in such a way that the first, middle, and final scenes of the book have as their common setting the scaffold or platform of the town pillory. We are now in the middle of the story. The previous chapter had ended with an effective bit of suspense, as we are told that Dimmesdale had a sudden thought, "stole softly down the staircase, undid the door, and issued forth."

Dimmesdale's idea is to make a confession of his adultery, cowardice, and cover-up, so he mounts the scaffold by night. Because "there was no peril of discovery," the vigil (as Hawthorne terms it) is of course ineffectual in relieving Dimmesdale's guilt. Nonetheless, it is one of the most vividly realized scenes in the whole book. As Rev. Wilson passes by after attending the governor on his deathbed, Dimmesdale imagines that he greeted his fellow clergyman. Then Dimmesdale fantasizes a scene in which he becomes paralyzed on the platform and is viewed the next morning by the townspeople.

For vivid descriptive writing, it is hard to beat this chapter. Hawthorne's visual imagination was working overtime as he composed it.

An aura of defeat hovers over the action in this chapter. Dimmesdale undertakes his experiment in high hopes, but the venture is doomed from the start. "There was no peril of discovery," we read. For that very reason, the "confession" is, in the words of the text, a "mockery of penitence." A good strategy for working one's way through the chapter is to list the items that make the action a litany of things that doom Dimmesdale's attempt to find relief.

In this action-packed scene, Hester and Pearl suddenly appear and converse with Dimmesdale. In fact, they ascend the platform, and Dimmesdale takes Pearl by the hand, experiencing "what seemed a tumultuous rush of new life." This is followed by the appearance of a light in the sky (a touch of the supernatural in this romance), a portent in the form of the letter A. The guilt-haunted Dimmesdale interprets it as an accusing letter A for adultery (though the public verdict is that it stands for Angel, to accompany the governor to heaven at the moment of his death).

Finally Roger Chillingworth passes by and leads the despondent Dimmesdale home. When Dimmesdale asks who Chillingworth really is, Hester remains silent, an act that further dooms Dimmesdale to being a victim of Chillingworth's manipulation. The next day Dimmesdale preaches his most effective gospel sermon ever, and as he descends from the pulpit the sexton hands him his glove that had been found on the scaffold.

Commentary

We can begin by placing this chapter into its literary family. *The Scarlet Letter* is a story of crime and punishment. A familiar literary convention in such stories is that the criminal has an impulse to return to the scene of the crime. In this case the crime is not the original adultery but the crime of silence and cover-up that occurred when Dimmesdale refused to stand with Hester on the scaffold as the father of Pearl. Of course there is psychological realism in the literary convention: even in real life, criminals return to the scene of the crime because they are consumed with guilt over what they did.

The conventions of the suspense story also

Hawthorne's impulse to develop his story by means of symbolism is fully evident in this chapter. Mistress Hibbins and Roger Chillingworth are associated with images of witches and demons. The text itself equates "the minister, with his hand over his heart; and Hester Prynne, with the embroidered letter glimmering on her bosom; and little Pearl, herself a symbol." The light of the meteor is interpreted in alternate ways as a symbol.

Modern readers might wonder why Hawthorne's story accepts the premise that Dimmesdale's confession must be public instead of merely personal, between the sinner and his God. Dimmesdale's sins of adultery, cover-up, and hypocrisy are social in their nature and ramifications, so in the very nature of the situation confession needs to be public.

enter the action. Hawthorne composes the story in such a way that once Dimmesdale mounts the scaffold we wonder from moment to moment what will happen. Will he be discovered? Will the secret come out? The suspense story becomes a story of discovery as well, as we come to see that Dimmesdale will never recover until he makes a public confession of his sins of adultery and hypocrisy. As the story unfolds, Dimmesdale's situation becomes increasingly terrible, as he fills the role of the archetypal man with a problem that will not go away. Perhaps the most important aspect of the chapter is the foreshadowing of future action that it contains. We do not yet know it, but when Dimmesdale, Hester, and Pearl stand on the platform holding each other's hands we are being given a preview of the main action that will occur at the climax of the story. The "new life" that Dimmesdale experiences as he grasps Pearl's hands is a premonition of Dimmesdale's conversion in the final confession scene. When Pearl asks in her childish naivety whether the three will stand on this site "to-morrow noontide," Dimmesdale replies that they will stand together "one other day, but not to-morrow." When pressed to explain, Dimmesdale says, "At the great judgment day." Irony pervades the statement, since the great judgment day will turn out to be the fast-approaching last day of Dimmesdale's life, not the last day of human history.

The chief contribution of this inspired piece of writing to the overall plot is that it is a landmark in the life of Dimmesdale (who by now has become the protagonist of the story). The story as a whole is structured as a problem that requires a solution. The problem is Dimmesdale's unrelieved guilt and

> "The story moves along with the rhythm of a detective thriller, quickening as its network of suspicion tightens and is confirmed. Hester and Chillingworth recognize each other at the commencement; Chillingworth recognizes Dimmesdale by the middle of the book; and Dimmesdale Chillingworth midway through the second half."—Harry Levin, "Introduction," *The Scarlet Letter*

the ruin that it has brought into his life. In this chapter an attempted solution to the problem is eliminated as a possibility. We increasingly sense that only a genuine confession made in public can solve Dimmesdale's problem.

For Reflection or Discussion

The literature of the world, from the story of Cain in Genesis 4 to the latest television crime drama, is laden with the motifs of an attempted cover-up of a crime and the criminal's return to the scene of the crime (or, in a variation, the guilty person's saying too much to the detective); what are some examples? In addition, how does the plot in this chapter generate suspense as it unfolds? Where are irony, foreshadowing, and symbolism exerted?

CHAPTER 13

Another View of Hester

Plot Summary

The story of Hester is the story of suffering and isolated humanity. But it is a rule of storytelling that a character's situation changes and develops. The purpose of this chapter in Hester's development (seven years after the beginning of the story) is a kind of progress report. The previous chapter had narrated the worsening situation of Dimmesdale; this chapter narrates the improving situation of Hester.

To accentuate the "progress report" nature of the material, the storyteller does all of the talking in this chapter. Instead of narrating action, he offers an assessment and summary of action.

Storytellers love to work by contrast and juxtaposition. After several chapters that have unfolded the ongoing story of Dimmesdale, this chapter shifts the focus back to Hester. The story of Dimmesdale's downward plunge is now countered by an account of Hester's ascent over her earlier ostracism. Dimmesdale moves in a world of Puritan practice and Christian doctrine; in this chapter Hester's Romantic worldview is firmly established.

Several archetypal plot motifs are just below the surface in this chapter. The label "another view of Hester" places Hester's changing status in the category of transformation story. Hester's changing social situation makes this a change of fortune story. But Hester's drift from a Puritan/Christian worldview to a Romantic worldview makes her story a change of character story as well. The rescue story enters our awareness when Hester in the last paragraph of the chapter resolves to confront Chillingworth and effect "the rescue of the victim on whom he had so evidently set his gripe."

If we exert a sufficiently strong interpretive hand on the material, we can view the contrast between Dimmesdale's decline and Hester's ascent as a contrast between concealed sin and revealed sin.

The key interpretive statement within the chapter was so important to Hawthorne that he placed it all by itself as a one-sentence paragraph: "The scarlet letter had not done its office." The most obvious meaning is that Hester's punish-

There are two main aspects to the report. One is Hester's external standing in the community. Hester is so helpful to people in need that the A on her breast has actually changed its meaning in the eyes of the public, no longer representing "adultery" but rather "able."

The second entry in Hester's "file" focuses not on her external standing in the community but in the interior of her mind and spirit. In a single packed paragraph two-thirds of the way through the chapter, Hawthorne develops a portrait of Hester as the arch-Romanticist.

With the subject announced in the title finished, Hawthorne turns at the end of the chapter to action. Spurred on by what Hester had seen on the night of Dimmesdale's ineffectual vigil on the scaffold, Hester resolves to break her silence regarding Chillingworth's true identity.

Commentary

The key to interpreting this chapter (as with many chapters in *The Scarlet Letter*) lies in the title of the chapter. In this chapter we receive "another view of Hester." Exploring exactly what is meant by that label is the chief interpretive task.

At one level, the new woman who emerges in this chapter is a success story. It is, as the narrator calls it, the story of "a woman's strength." As readers, we become a silent cheering section as we see Hester deservedly win acceptance in the very community that had tormented her. Our joy is tempered by realism, as Hawthorne devotes a whole long paragraph to delineating the loss of a certain exuberance, as well as physical attractiveness, in Hester. Even here there is a subtle note of foreshadowing, as we are told that Hester, who has at one level ceased to be a woman, might with a "magic touch" be transformed back into a woman; this looks forward to the eventual decision of Hester and Dimmesdale to flee from Boston.

The more subtle "new" Hester relates to the fullest revelation yet of Hester's adherence to a Romantic worldview. Hawthorne was writing at the high tide of nineteenth-century Romanticism. In a key paragraph, Hawthorne describes the Romantic spirit of the revolutionary new world view and then asserts, "Hester Prynne imbibed this spirit." The ramifications of this will occupy the rest of the story.

For Reflection or Discussion

The two most important interpretive issues are stated right in the text. What things constitute the "other view of Hester" that emerges in this chapter? Second, in what ways is the case that "the scarlet letter had not done its office"?

ment by the Puritan community led her to outward conformity but not inward conviction. In contrast to Dimmesdale, who fully embraces Christian doctrine, Hester becomes a Romanticist in her convictions, as later action will disclose.

In a chapter that flaunts Romantic sentiments, the narrator continues to include asides that keep our awareness of a Christian worldview alive. For example, he speaks of "the iron link of mutual crime" that neither Hester nor Dimmesdale "could break." Again, Pearl's "own nature had something wrong in it, which continually betokened that she had been born amiss—the effluence of her mother's lawless passion."

CHAPTER 14

Hester and the Physician

Plot Summary

Hester follows through on the resolve introduced at the end of the previous chapter: she confronts her husband Roger Chillingworth regarding his victimizing of Dimmesdale. It is a dramatized scene in which dialogue carries the story. In particular, Hester wants release from the promise (made seven years earlier when Chillingworth attended Hester in her prison cell) not to disclose

This chapter belongs to an important category of literature known as the "story of intercession." In such a story, a character undertakes a process of appealing to another character to change a course of action for the benefit of a third party. Such stories are always stories of persuasion. Part of our attention flows toward the resourcefulness of the intercessor's reasons why the other person should relent, and part of our attention flows to the response of the person who must decide whether to relent. This chapter is one of the great intercession scenes in literature. Biblical examples include Abraham's intercession on behalf of Lot; Moses on behalf of the wayward Israelites; Abigail on behalf of her husband, Nabal; Esther on behalf of her nation.

Archetypes abound in this chapter. Chillingworth is the archetypal fiend. His relationship to Dimmesdale is based on the revenge motif. The description of Chillingworth is managed in such a way as to paint a picture of transformation. When given the opportunity to extend mercy, Chillingworth becomes the archetypal refuser of festivities, in the mold of Shakespeare's villain Shylock, who refuses to extend mercy to someone in his debt.

"The greatness of *The Scarlet Letter* lies in the character of Hester Prynne. . . . She achieved spiritual greatness in spite of her own human weakness, in spite of the prejudices of her Puritan society."
—F. I. Carpenter, "Scarlet A Minus"

Chillingworth's identity to Dimmesdale. Hester makes an appeal that Chillingworth relent in his revenge against Dimmesdale, and Chillingworth refuses.

Commentary

A main focus of the chapter is the degenerating character of Chillingworth. The previous chapter gave us "another view of Hester"; this chapter gives us another view of Chillingworth. Demonic imagery is repeatedly applied to Chillingworth and becomes a chief means of characterizing him. As part of this pattern, Chillingworth is several times referred to as "the old man"—old as Satan, the implication is.

If Chillingworth belongs to the archetype of the fiend, he is also an example of character type that can be traced all the way back to ancient Greek comedy. It is known as the refuser of festivities. Hester offers Chillingworth the opportunity "to pardon," which she immediately labels a "privilege" and "priceless benefit." The bitter old man replies, "It is not granted me to pardon. . . . Now go thy ways." In other words, Chillingworth has refused to participate in a great drama of forgiveness that is made available to him.

Additionally, the language of torture and torment is prominent in the conversation between Hester and Chillingworth. For example, Hester asks, "Hast thou not tortured him enough?" The torture is part of the revenge motif in the story—a story of "perpetual poison of the direst revenge."

For Reflection or Discussion

Storytelling is an affective art in which storytellers convey what they have to say by getting readers to feel a certain way toward characters and events in the story. A good way to make sense of this chapter is to monitor and name the feelings that are elicited by details as we keep reading.

CHAPTER 15

Hester and Pearl

Plot Summary

Good stories are based on the principle of rhythm—a back-and-forth flow between two poles. After the intensity of Hester's encounter with Chillingworth in the previous chapter, where Hester attempts to get her husband to relent in his hatred toward Dimmesdale, this chapter is a low-voltage one. It is partly a transition from Hester's encounter with Chillingworth to her encounter with Dimmesdale. The main narrative business of chapter 15 is to bring us up to date on the development of Pearl. We mainly see a reinforcement of tendencies of Pearl's character that had been established early in the story.

Commentary

We can trust Hawthorne to signal what he regards as most important to his designs in *The Scarlet Letter*. The villainous character of Chillingworth and his degeneration into an increasingly terrifying figure of evil is not just a plot device but an important part of Hawthorne's moral vision. Accordingly, the first fifth of this chapter is a follow-up to Hester's encounter with Chillingworth, and as we listen to Hester talk within herself, the true horror

As Hawthorne lays it on with the demonic villainy of Chillingworth, we can scarcely avoid asking what role villains play in the storyteller's craft. They embody the evil that we know exists in the world, thereby doing justice to our own experiences and fears. In other words, villains belong to the realm of literary realism. Often they are heightened beyond what we find in real life, but it is in the nature of the literary imagination to heighten experiences so we can see them more clearly. Of course literature is a mirror as well as a window, so that we can see something of ourselves in literary villains. Finally, villains simply add a lot of interest to a story. They elicit strong reader involvement, which is a high goal of any storyteller.

Here are chapter titles from *The Scarlet Letter*: "The Elf-Child and the Minister"; "The Leech and His Patient"; "Hester and the Physician"; "Hester and Pearl"; "The Pastor and His Parishioner." Obviously one of Hawthorne's favorite strategies is to segregate pairs of characters and let them interact with each other. This shows that one of Hawthorne's skills was a genius for drama, in the sense of character interaction by means of dialogue.

The key to the characterization of Pearl in the book as a whole is her ambivalence. She is partly good and partly bad. If she brings joy to her mother, she is also an agent of retribution. The latter motif dominates this chapter.

"The Scarlet Letter, like all very great fiction, is the product of a controlled division of sympathies. . . . It has always been possible to remark, about Hawthorne, his fondness for the dusky places. . . . But it has also been possible to read *The Scarlet Letter* . . . as an endorsement of hopefulness."
—R. W. B. Lewis, *The American Adam*

of Chillingworth as a figure of evil is allowed to register with us.

From the beginning, Pearl has been a child of nature, and a figment of the Romantic imagination—elf-like and more than human. Those facets of her characterization are strongly reinforced in this chapter. What is new is Pearl's emerging awareness of the symbolic A that her mother wears on her breast.

In fact, Pearl's questioning her mother about the A, accompanied by her own statements about it, constitutes the second half of this chapter. At the beginning of the story, the A had stood for adultery. When Pearl claims that her mother wears the A "for the same reason that the minister keeps his hand over his heart," a new element enters the story. Earlier the symbolic gesture of the hand over the heart had implied guilt, concealment, and psychic and physical decline. Now it becomes an index to Pearl's growing awareness.

For Reflection or Discussion
The opening paragraphs in which Hester ponders her feelings about Chillingworth (including her hatred of him) provide a good occasion to reach some final conclusions about the role of Chillingworth in the story, and in particular why Hawthorne regarded him as such an important part of the book. Regarding Pearl, the chief character in this chapter, what things make her an example of nineteenth-century Romanticism? What is Pearl's role in Hester's life?

CHAPTER 16

A Forest Walk

Plot Summary

This chapter is an extension of the previous chapter. The two characters on stage are still Hester and Pearl. The characterization of Pearl continues to be a dominant motif. The conversation between mother and child continues to show Pearl's growing awareness—this time as it pertains to Chillingworth rather than Dimmesdale. Pearl's questions and statements not only show her growing perceptiveness about what is happening in the adult world around her; in effect she becomes a commentator on the action—a travel guide to what is happening. There is thus plenty to engage our interest in this chapter, but its function in the plot is simple: it sets the stage for a momentous conversation between Hester and Dimmesdale in the next chapter.

A touch of romance fantasy that appears in this chapter is so memorable that it sticks in the memory even though its relation to the plot is minimal. In the forest, the sunlight keeps shining on Pearl as she flits about, while at the same time avoiding Hester.

Commentary

It is a truism that Hawthorne made the great symbols of *The Scarlet Letter* ambiguous and ambivalent. He did it, moreover, with images and symbols that in the Romantic worldview of his day were simple. This chapter highlights the complexity of some of Hawthorne's symbols.

We can begin with the forest. For Romanticism, the forest was a phenomenon of nature and

Hawthorne is so famous as a symbolist that it would be possible to overlook his expertise at realistic description of scenes and characters. This chapter affords the usual quota of opportunities to relish Hawthorne's descriptive ability. At points he rises to the status of nature writer.

Another forte of Hawthorne's is his ability to express childhood psychology. The portrayal of Pearl in this chapter, with her mingled childish naivety and perceptiveness beyond her years, affords good examples.

therefore the repository of goodness. It represented freedom from the restraints of civilization and society. The forest in *The Scarlet Letter* partly adheres to this pattern. It is in the forest that Hester and Dimmesdale in the next chapter will formulate a dream of freedom and escape. Pearl's natural innocence, symbolized by her ability to "catch the sunshine" that follows her everywhere, is part of the symbolism.

But there is more to the forest than this. The narrator tells us that "to Hester's mind, it imaged not amiss the moral wilderness in which she had so long been wandering." As we will see in the next chapter, the freedom of the forest does not become reality for Hester and Dimmesdale, as encapsulated in Hester's comment that "the forest cannot hide" Hester's A.

Although this chapter does not bring the village into the picture, this is a good place to consider the ambivalence of the town—civilization and society—in *The Scarlet Letter*. In the Romantic paradigm, the city was the repository of human evil—the absence of nature and natural feeling and virtue. This is part of the truth about the Boston of *The Scarlet Letter*, inasmuch as it is the place of social oppression. But the town, and not the forest, is the place of Christian belief, and it is there that Dimmesdale will achieve the salvation of his soul.

Another symbol that becomes complex in this chapter is the Black Man. Throughout the story up to this point, the Black Man of the forest has been identified with Satan and sometimes by extension with Chillingworth. But in this chapter Hester says, "Once in my life I met the Black Man! . . . This scarlet letter is his mark!" Is the Black Man Dimmesdale too?

Throughout the book Hawthorne drops isolated statements of foreshadowing into the text. On a first reading, we could not possibly know what they are pointing to. One of the most evocative of these statements of foreshadowing occurs in this chapter. Regarding Pearl we read, "She wanted [lacked] . . . a grief that should deeply touch her, and thus humanize her and make her capable of sympathy. But there was time enough for little Pearl!" It will all come to fruition in the climactic scene of the book.

For Reflection or Discussion

A good approach to the chapter is to explore the stated or implied ambivalence (duality) of Pearl and the forest. Second, images of evil such as Mistress Hibbins and the Black Man move in and out of the chapter; tracing these image patterns yields a lot. What does the story say by means of these images of evil?

CHAPTER 17

The Pastor and His Parishioner

Plot Summary

The entire preceding chapter ("A Forest Walk") was a buildup to an emotion-packed encounter between Hester and Dimmesdale. Hester's avowed purpose in seeking an occasion for the encounter was to break her silence to Dimmesdale regarding who Chillingworth really is. But the conversation leads to greater things than the disclosure of a secret.

After a masterful evocation of atmosphere, Hawthorne recounts the conversation between Hester and Dimmesdale. In other words, as so often, his method of proceeding is that of drama. The conversation unfolds in four phases. (1) Dimmesdale responds to Hester's version of the question "How are you doing?" with a statement of his extreme misery. (2) Hester reveals Chillingworth's identity and pleads with Dimmesdale for his forgiveness of her for concealing the truth. (3) Now that the ground rules have changed, the question arises as to what course of action should be pursued. (4) Hester proposes that she and Dimmes-

Hawthorne has already shown his fondness for ironic titles, and here he springs another one on us. "The Pastor and His Parishioner" names the external social roles of Dimmesdale and Hester. But the public relationship of these two sexual partners hardly gets at the heart of the matter. A related irony is that ordinarily a pastor counsels a parishioner; Dimmesdale reverses that role when he says to Hester, "Advise me what to do."

dale flee from the society that has tormented them and "begin all anew!"

Commentary

The profundity of issues heats up in this chapter, far in excess of the simplicity of the plot summary provided above. The momentousness of what is happening is underscored by the "mood writing" that precedes the conversation. The writing is magical and otherworldly, as the couple meets in a manner like "the first encounter, in the world beyond the grave, of two spirits who had been intimately connected in their former life, but now stood coldly shuddering, in mutual dread."

The key to interpreting the chapter is the essentially Romantic nature of what the couple decides to do under the prompting of Hester. This Romanticism is set over against a Christian viewpoint, as exemplified by Dimmesdale. In reply to the question of whether she has found peace, Hester looks at the A that she wears on her breast. In other words, evil is external and societal. By contrast, Dimmesdale speaks of the "spiritual torment" with which he lives as a guilty sinner. The contrast is partly a contrast between revealed and concealed sin, but it is also a contrast between Romantic and Christian worldviews.

The conflict between Romantic and Christian keeps surfacing in this chapter. For the Romanticist Hester, "what we did had a consecration of its own. We felt it so!" The contrary viewpoint is represented by Dimmesdale: "'The judgment of God is on me,' answered the conscience-stricken priest." Hester the Romanticist suffers no pangs of conscience; for her, evil is the ostracism she has suffered at the hands of her society.

We need to give proper weight to the vocabulary that Hester uses when proposing her dream of an escape. For example, she first proposes escaping westward into the wilderness, where there is "no vestige of the white man's tread." If there is no white man's influence, there is no Christianity. Similarly, "What hast thou to do with all these iron men, and their opinions?" For all the unsavory behavior that goes on in Puritan Boston, the opinions that prevail are the truths of the Christian faith.

The Romantic and Christian views not only differ in their diagnosis of the problem; they also differ in their solutions. For Hester, since the problem lies in external society, not in the guilty soul of the individual, the solution is simple, namely, escape from the society that torments the couple. "There thou art free!" exclaims Hester. For Dimmesdale, the problem is not external and societal: "Lost as my soul is," he says at one point.

Of course we do not yet know how the story will resolve this conflict that it sets up between Romantic and Christian worldviews. We will not know that until the story is finished. In the next chapter the story will momentarily get us to feel positively toward the plan to escape.

For Reflection or Discussion

The worldview issues that are raised are tremendous, but before becoming overly intellectual in analyzing this chapter it is important to be receptive to the abundance of human experience that is embodied. What human experiences and feelings are we asked to share as the chapter unfolds? Having been duly moved by what transpires, we need to disentangle the worldview issues. Where does a Romantic outlook get expressed? Where a Christian outlook?

In response to Dimmesdale's defeatist statement, "The judgment of God is on me. . . . It is too mighty for me to struggle with," literary critic Joseph Schwartz writes that Dimmesdale's "fundamental weakness is not his sin, nor even his hypocrisy, but his failure to recognize that God is a God of love. . . . He cannot understand the nature of Him Whom he has offended . . . . His moral decline runs parallel with his confusion about God. . . . His topic is always the horror of sin and the terror of hell. Hopelessness has made the topic of salvation impossible." All of this will be reversed in the conversion scene with which the story ends.

CHAPTER 18

A Flood of Sunshine

Plot Summary

The previous chapter ended like a chapter in a serial publication, leaving the reader wondering what would happen next. All we were told is that Dimmesdale was enraptured by the thought of escaping with Hester. The function of chapter 18 is to instill in the reader a sympathetic attitude toward the decision to escape.

That persuasive strategy starts with the title: "A Flood of Sunshine." Thereafter the narrator shuttles back and forth among three types of material. Sometimes he provides context and commentary for the action that is happening (see commentary section below). Sometimes he quotes the dialogue that transpired between Hester and Dimmesdale. And a few times he narrates action, as when Hester removes the A from her breast and removes the cap from her head to let her hair flow down, and when Hester summons Pearl.

Commentary

The varied types of material that flow together in this scene (see plot summary above) are all governed by a single purpose—to make the reader feel positively toward the decision to escape. A tone of exhilaration permeates the chapter.

The commentary with which the narrator explains what is happening accentuates that the decision is based on the premises of a Romantic worldview. The key statement (but not the only one) is this: the liberation that the couple feels is that "of breathing the wild, free atmosphere of an unredeemed, unchristianized, lawless region." In the Romantic view, the couple's problem is not an inner guilt that needs forgiveness but simply the oppressiveness of society.

The key sentence in this regard is Hester's comment after she has removed the A from her breast that "with this symbol, I undo it all, and

The two halves of *The Scarlet Letter* are both structured as a pyramid, with the action building toward an emotional high in the middle of each half and then descending back into sad events. Chapter 18 is the peak of emotional exuberance in the second half of the book. For the moment, everything seems to be heading in the right direction for Hester and Dimmesdale.

Hester's Romantic outlook is strongly reinforced in this chapter. Everything that she says and does is an expression of all that nineteenth-century Romantics advocated. The commentary of the narrator confirms that Hester is a heroine in the Romantic mold. Even in her characterization, though, the narrator gives hints of the Christian viewpoint that subverts Hester's Romanticism. For example, the narrator tells us that Hester "had wandered, without rule or guidance, in a moral wilderness."

make it as it had never been!" Christianity claims that sin produces inner guilt that only God's forgiveness can remove and make as if it had never been. Romanticism rejects that premise and believes that removing oneself from external social disapproval is sufficient to "make it as it had never been."

Another leading purpose of Hawthorne is to highlight Hester and Dimmesdale as foils to each other. Hester the Romanticist has been waiting for this moment all along: "As regarded Hester Prynne, the whole seven years of outlaw and ignominy had been little other than a preparation for this very hour." By contrast, the text belabors the point that Dimmesdale is Christian in his convictions. He is entering new territory in agreeing to Hester's plan of escape. To render the situation even more complex, as Dimmesdale embraces the Romantic decision he does so in standard Christian terminology: "Of a deeply religious temperament, there was inevitably a tinge of the devotional in his mood." For example, he says, "Neither can I any longer live without her [Hester's] companionship: so powerful is she to sustain—so tender to soothe! O Thou to whom I dare not lift mine eyes, wilt Thou yet pardon me!"

The larger interpretive question, of course, is how the story as a whole gets us to feel about this momentary ecstasy. That question will be answered in the chapters that follow, but we get premonitions already in this chapter that Hester's grand Romantic experiment will be defeated—first by reality, then by a Christian view of things. The narrator says in this chapter, "And be the stern and sad truth spoken, that the breach which guilt has once made into the human soul is never, in this

> Hawthorne does not belabor the fact that the decision to escape runs counter to Christian values, but he plants a few very clear "flags" that alert us to that fact. One of them is this: "Such was the sympathy of Nature—that wild, heathen Nature of the forest, never subjugated by human law, nor illuminated by higher truth—with the bliss of these two spirits!" The "higher truth" is supernatural revelation, or the Bible and its teachings.

The characterization of Dimmesdale is the most complex aspect of this chapter. Reader-response literary criticism encourages readers to bring their own convictions into the reading and interpretation of literature. Christian readers have reason to know that Dimmesdale "has it all wrong" when he utters the following: "O Hester, thou art my better angel! I seem to have flung myself—sick, sin-stained, and sorrow-blackened—down upon these forest-leaves, and to have risen up all made anew, and with new powers to glorify Him that hath been merciful! This is already the better life!" For readers who cannot bring that degree of Christian allegiance to the text, the negative verdict on Dimmesdale will need to wait for later chapters of the story.

mortal state, repaired." In other words, sin brings inevitable consequences.

What happens in this chapter fits into Hawthorne's strategy (which many storytellers have used) of the guilty reader. As readers we are swept into the excitement and attractiveness of the moment. Everything seems to be positive in the actions of Hester and Dimmesdale. Later the story will persuade us in the opposite direction, but for the moment we have been guilty readers, approving an action that is wrong. We have become participants in the moral action of the story, falling as Dimmesdale does.

For Reflection or Discussion

The main interpretive task is to record and simply experience the ways in which the chapter generates sympathy and enthusiasm for what Hester and Dimmesdale say and do as the chapter unfolds. Within the sheer abundance of data, what stands out as the most moving pieces of data? Moving beyond the affective level, what details make it clear that the decision is based on Romantic standards? Even more subtly, what latent signs bring a Christian worldview into view as a counter to the exuberant Romanticism?

CHAPTER 19

The Child at the Brook-Side

Plot Summary

The previous chapter, too, ended with the "to be continued" motif of stories that are published serially. Hester had summoned Pearl in hopes that she would accept Dimmesdale as her father. The parting shot had been that Pearl "came slowly back. Slowly; for she saw the clergyman!" What does that mean? Chapter 19 tells us.

Chapter 19 is the counterpoint to chapter 18. One chapter takes us to an emotional high; the other catapults us down to an emotional low. The action is simplicity personified: Pearl totally rejects the possibility of claiming Dimmesdale as a father. She points accusingly at Dimmesdale and shrieks. When Dimmesdale kisses her, she runs to the brook and washes off the kiss. Hester has no alternative but to restore the A to her bosom and tie her hair up again. The final paragraph brings the chapter to a totally despondent close.

Commentary

The function of this chapter is to counter the mood of the previous chapter. The previous chapter created a mood of exuberant celebration over the decision to escape. This chapter casts that decision in a negative light. Exactly what defeats the dream of a new life? In this chapter, reality defeats the dream. Pearl, who in an earlier chapter had been called the scarlet letter in a living form, makes it impossible for her parents simply to run away from the life they brought upon themselves by their adultery. She possesses the quality of retribution in the lives of Hester and Dimmesdale.

The narrator drives the point home. He tells us that Hester received the scarlet letter back "from the hand of fate." In other words, there is an inevitability about the death of the dream of escape. The narrator says further, "So it ever is, whether thus typified or no, that an evil deed invests itself with the character of doom."

Characters in stories undertake experiments in living. They pursue their experiment to its logical conclusion. This conclusion has the quality of an outcome. That outcome, moreover, is a device of disclosure by which the storytellers tip their hand in regard to the values and worldview that they intend to affirm. If the experiment comes to a positive conclusion, the story can be said to endorse the worldview embodied in the experiment. Contrariwise, if a character's experiment in living ends in defeat, the storyteller thereby signals disapproval of the worldview implied by the experiment.

The fact that literary characters undertake experiments in living imposes a twofold task on readers. One is to determine the exact nature of the experiment that a given character undertakes. The other is to identify what the outcome of the experiment says about what the author of the story is offering for the reader's approval. Hester and Dimmesdale's plan to escape from New England to Europe is a Romantic experiment, based on the premise that the problem requiring a solution is the oppressiveness of the Puritan society in which they live. As reality and (later) Christian premises defeat this Romantic dream, we see part of Hawthorne's worldview in this book. Chapter 19 renders a provisional verdict that the Romantic dream does not adequately take reality into account.

"The book . . . is concerned with 'the wages of sin.' Unlike modern writers, Hawthorne is not so concerned with what causes sin as with what sin causes. . . . What makes Hawthorne's consideration of guilt and its effect so appealing to modern readers is its psychological validity." —John C. Gerber, *Twentieth Century Interpretations of The Scarlet Letter*

Hester, however, is not fully perceptive. In the most evocative statement of the chapter, she says that "the forest cannot hide it," in acknowledgment that simply escaping from the town to the forest cannot remove the letter and what it symbolizes. But then she immediately reverts to her Romantic illusion: "The mid-ocean shall take it from my hand, and swallow it up for ever!"

For Reflection or Discussion

Storytelling is a calculated strategy of controlling a reader's emotions; what feelings are evoked as the chapter unfolds? How do those emotions fit into the ongoing flow of the story? How does this chapter fit into Hawthorne's technique of the guilty reader?

CHAPTER 20

The Minister in a Maze

Plot Summary

The knell of doom was so strong at the end of the previous chapter that we could easily be lulled into thinking that the planned escape has been abandoned. But the trip is still on, to our surprise. We are even given a glimpse of the itinerary: it will be a journey by ship to the Old World (presumably England). The day of embarkation will be the day after Election Day, when Dimmesdale will preach his farewell sermon.

Chapter 20 is a triumph of psychological insight (a Hawthorne forte). The chapter takes us inside Dimmesdale's mind as he tries to negotiate the new secret that he harbors and the need to discharge his everyday duties as a minister. Latent humor even enters the story for the first time. When Dimmesdale meets a deacon, he scarcely avoids uttering a blasphemy. He cannot recall a biblical verse on the immortality of the soul to a recently widowed parishioner. He is tempted to say something evil to a young woman of the church and to utter improper jests to others. Of course the text itself tells us how to interpret these actions (see commentary section below).

The climax of the chapter comes when, as Dimmesdale is preparing his Election Day sermon, Chillingworth enters the study. When "old [that is, satanic] Roger Chillingworth" enters the room, "the minister stood, white and speechless, with one hand on the Hebrew Scriptures, and the other spread upon his breast." As with a camera click, we see the divided soul of Arthur Dimmesdale, suspended between Christian conviction and the experience of guilt. Dimmesdale renounces his need for Chillingworth's medical oversight of his life. In a flurry of impulse, Dimmesdale throws his sermon into the fire and writes an inspired new one.

Commentary

What is going on in this psychological melodrama? Hawthorne clues us in. First, the minister is "in a maze" or trance because he is attempting to live in two worlds at the same time. Maybe he even dissociates, leaving this world for a fantasy world. Here is how Hawthorne as travel guide to the story puts it: "No man, for any considerable period, can wear one face to himself, and another to the multitude, without finally getting bewildered as to which may be the true." What follows from this principle is

The Scarlet Letter is not exactly a detective story, but it has many affinities with that genre. Being a story of crime and punishment, the story naturally lavishes attention on the criminal mind. One of the conventions of the detective story, whether in real life or fiction, is that the criminals seek to avoid detection at the conscious level but are betrayed by their subconscious into calling attention to themselves with suspicious behavior. In this chapter, Dimmesdale is betrayed by his subconscious.

The narrator offers this explanation for Dimmesdale's behavior: the sinful decision made in the forest "had stupefied all blessed impulses, and awakened into vivid life the whole brotherhood of bad ones." Romans 7:19 is a good interpretive lens through which to view what is happening: "For I do not do the good I want, but the evil I do not want is what I keep on doing." In the climax of that passage, Paul calls himself a "wretched man" (v. 24); the narrator calls Dimmesdale "the wretched minister."

The action in this chapter combines psychological and spiritual threads of action. The underlying premise is that the aberrant behavior of the protagonist is the psychological outworking of a spiritual problem. Two classic stories of English literature are possible sources for Hawthorne, and in any case they provide good parallels. In the sleepwalking scene in Shakespeare's *Macbeth*, Lady Macbeth's actions combine the moral and psychological aspects of guilt. So, too, in Samuel Coleridge's *Rime of the Ancient Mariner*, where the voyage of the mariner is at once a psychological and spiritual voyage into evil and guilt.

that "before Mr. Dimmesdale reached home [from the forest meeting with Hester], his inner man gave him other evidences of a revolution in the sphere of thought and feeling. In truth, nothing short of a total change of dynasty and moral code, in that interior kingdom, was adequate to account for the impulses now communicated to the unfortunate and startled minister."

That is the psychological level of action. The spiritual level runs parallel to it. As Dimmesdale himself tries to understand the voice that tempts him to improper behavior, he finally asks himself, "Am I mad? Or am I given over utterly to the fiend. Did I make a contract with him in the forest, and sign it with my blood?" The narrator confirms that diagnosis: "The wretched minister! He had made a bargain very like it! Tempted by a dream of happiness, he had yielded himself with deliberate choice . . . to what he knew was deadly sin. And the infectious poison of that sin had been thus rapidly diffused throughout his moral system."

For Reflection or Discussion

The text tells us that "another man had returned out of the forest"; what are the dimensions and/or manifestations of the transformation that has overtaken Dimmesdale? What psychological insights are most noteworthy? The witch-like old Mistress Hibbins has flitted in and out of the action as a shadowy figure; as she makes a return appearance in this chapter, what conclusions should we reach about her characterization in the story and her contribution to it?

CHAPTER 21

The New England Holiday

Plot Summary

This chapter and the next are not self-contained; they exist to set up the eventual climax of the story—the confession scene that occurs on the scaffold on Election Day. As the title of this chapter hints, this chapter sets up the place and occasion for the climactic action. The Puritans in New England had the custom of holding numerous festivals and "days off" during the course of a year. Election Day—the day of voting for civil officials—was one of those days. Being devotees of sermons, the Puritans naturally made a sermon and public worship service part of the day's festivities.

Chapter 21 of *The Scarlet Letter* is as much a bit of social history as it is fictional narrative. A whole slice of life from seventeenth-century New England comes alive in our imaginations. Hawthorne's descriptive ability is at its best in the chapter.

Commentary

Hawthorne wants to pull out all the stops with the climactic chapter of his story. One way to do so is to set the stage for eventual action. It is important to Hawthorne's design that Dimmesdale's public confession be as public as possible. One effect of chapter 21 is that it fills the town of Boston with people. There will be no shortage of spectators at the confession scene.

Additionally, the confession scene will affirm Puritan/Christian doctrine and also the Puritan

After all the negative propaganda that Hawthorne has lavished on the Puritans up to this point, it is refreshing that for the most part he is historically accurate in his portrayal of them in this chapter. Although the Puritans called a halt to Catholic holidays and holy days, they themselves multiplied private and public days exempt from work. They frequently called thanksgiving days when they invited friends to their homes for private services and feasts. They observed fast days. They commemorated annual events like political elections, ordinations of ministers, lectures, training, commencement days of courts, graduation days from colleges, and weddings.

It is a convention of storytelling that the author will give elaborate attention to the place where an impending really big event is about to take place. Just as in the old battle stories the arming of the hero was an extension of the hero's importance, setting the stage for a crucial event in a story is part of the event itself. For example, in the story of the prophet Elijah's showdown with the prophets of Baal (1 Kings 18), we get a full account of the stage props for the ensuing action. In a performance of Shakespeare's *Hamlet*, lavish attention is devoted to the stage props and entrance of spectators before the final fencing match between Laertes and Hamlet. Chapter 21 serves a similar function in *the Scarlet Letter*.

Not many hints are dropped regarding the eventual confession of Dimmesdale, but a couple of questions asked by Pearl function as foreshadowings. "Will the minister be there?" she asks, "and will he hold out both his hands to me, as when thou ledst me to him from the brook-side?" Pearl also remarks, "A strange, sad man is he with his hand always over his heart!"

practice of the public confessional. Hawthorne needed some softening of his picture of the Puritans if he planned to endorse the Puritans at the end of his story. This chapter presents the Puritans in a prevailingly positive light. They are shown engaging in sports and smiling.

The chapter contains two tie-ins to the story as a whole. One is the role that Hester and Pearl play in the scene. They are once again portrayed as fringe figures, spectators rather than participants in the festivities. Pearl, moreover, is her usual spirited self. Second, the impending voyage of Hester and Dimmesdale is kept alive, and irony surrounds it. Hester is sure that the townspeople are about to look on her scarlet letter for the last time. She makes plans with the captain of the ship that will sail the next day, and in an ominous development the mariner informs her that Chillingworth has also made plans to be on the voyage and has, moreover, pictured himself as part of the travel party of Hester and Dimmesdale.

For Reflection or Discussion

What are the most noteworthy features of the social scene that Hawthorne portrays in this chapter? How does the effect mitigate the completely negative portrayal of Puritan society up to this point in the story? How are the earlier characterizations of Hester, Pearl, and Dimmesdale reinforced in this chapter? How do irony and foreshadowing lend plot energy to a chapter that is predominantly descriptive?

CHAPTER 22

The Procession

Plot Summary

Setting an elaborate stage for ensuing action is one way to prepare for a crucial event in a story. If the crucial event will be a public occasion to which people march, the storyteller *really* has it made. Hawthorne was fortunate in every way. Election Day festivals in Puritan New England always included a procession of dignitaries in formal attire to the place of the sermon and related political functions, and afterwards from church to the site of the festival.

The procession in chapter 22 unfolds in five phases. First Hawthorne lists the individuals and groups who made up the procession. Then we get a close-up of Dimmesdale in the procession, with emphasis on his unaccustomed vigor. Then suddenly the camera shifts to Hester in the group of onlookers, and we share the thoughts that ran through her mind on this momentous occasion. Next the narrator gives a brief account of Dimmesdale's sermon preached inside the church. Finally, and at unexpected length, Hawthorne gives an elaborate account of the unusual amount of staring that people in the marketplace gave to Hester's scarlet letter A.

Commentary

In stories and movies, the appearance of a procession exists for the sake of a buildup to something climactic in the next phase of the story. The Election Day procession in *The Scarlet Letter* creates a mounting sense of anticipation as we move

A procession of people entering a place preliminary to a main event occurring there is a favorite ploy of storytellers and playwrights. In the movie *Chariots of Fire*, the pregame Olympic procession of athletes from various nations creates a sense of anticipation for the competitions to follow. Before the final fencing match in Shakespeare's *Hamlet*, the dignitaries of the court march into the room and take their assigned places. Adducing examples of the technique will help make chapter 22 of *The Scarlet Letter* come alive.

Hawthorne has shown himself a master of irony throughout *The Scarlet Letter*. His powers of irony do not desert him in this chapter. He accentuates the contrast between appearance and reality by planting hints that although Dimmesdale is at the very peak of his external prominence in the community, he actually bears a terrible burden of guilt that might undo him at any moment. The community has no clue of Dimmesdale's sin, but Hester, Pearl, Mistress Hibbins, and we as readers are in on the secret. At the end of the chapter, Hawthorne highlights the contrast between "the sainted minister" and "the woman of the scarlet letter," but then adds a note of irony in the final sentence: "What imagination would . . . surmise that the same scorching stigma was on them both?"

The primary pattern of premonition in this chapter focuses on the very clear implication that Dimmesdale is about to be exposed as Hester's partner in adultery. But a more subtle level of premonition also exists. The next chapter will drive a wedge between Dimmesdale and Hester in regard to their divergent worldviews and ways of coping with the failure of the dreamed-for escape to materialize. If we look really closely at chapter 22, we can pick up signposts of a break in the apparent harmony between Hester and Dimmesdale. Here is a specimen sentence: "Her spirit sank with the idea that all must have been a delusion, and that, vividly as she had dreamed it, there could be no real bond betwixt the clergyman and herself."

toward the climactic event of the book. Nothing in this chapter exists for its own sake; the purpose of everything that Hawthorne chose to include is anticipatory. We can discern three threads that Hawthorne wove into the tapestry of the chapter.

One is the characterization of Dimmesdale. An early paragraph portrays him as unaccustomedly energetic in body but distracted in mind. Hawthorne also notes Dimmesdale's lack of acknowledgment of Hester on this occasion, an indifference that Hester experiences as Dimmesdale's "unsympathizing thoughts" of which "she could scarcely forgive him." The witch-like Mistress Hibbins makes veiled statements about Dimmesdale's guilt.

Second, Hawthorne brings Hester into the picture in such a way as to make her and Dimmesdale mighty foils to each other, especially in regard to their external social standing on this particular day. Dimmesdale is the center of attention as the one who preaches the Election Day sermon. By contrast, detail after detail accentuates the isolation of Hester in the community, as she emerges yet again as the archetypal outsider. Dimmesdale, we are told, "Stood, at this moment, on the very proudest eminence of superiority." Hawthorne's parting shot in the chapter highlights the contrast: "The sainted minister in the church! The woman of the scarlet letter in the market-place!"

More important than anything else is the masterful way in which Hawthorne creates a sense of ominous premonition in this chapter. Pearl asks if Dimmesdale is the same person who had kissed her in the forest and then adds, "I could not be sure that it was he; so strange he looked." Mistress Hibbins tells Pearl that "thou shalt know wherefore the minister keeps his hand over his heart!" Hawthorne makes much of the plaintive undertone in Dimmesdale's voice as he delivers his sermon—an undertone that perhaps is "the complaint of a human heart, sorrow-laden, perchance guilty, telling its secret."

For Reflection or Discussion

What important aspects do we discern regarding the characterization of Dimmesdale? How are Dimmesdale and Hester portrayed as foils to each other in this chapter? What moments of foreshadowing and premonition do we experience as the chapter unfolds?

CHAPTER 23

The Revelation of the Scarlet Letter

Plot Summary

The first third of the chapter continues in the same vein as the previous chapter. We learn more about Dimmesdale's sermon. We receive still more assurance of Dimmesdale's exalted position in the eyes of the community at the present moment. There are more premonitions that something momentous is about to happen. The transition occurs as the procession leaves the church toward the festival.

Everything changes in a moment when Dimmesdale reaches the by-now famous scaffold or platform in the middle of town. The scene that follows is strongly dramatic in nature, with lavish

Everything is heightened in this chapter, and we need to be receptive to that heightening. Dimmesdale was not simply at a high point of his career as a minister—he "stood, at this moment, on the very proudest eminence of superiority." He has preached not simply a good sermon but a sermon that by "the united testimony" of the listeners was so exalted that "never had man spoken in so wise, so high, and so holy a spirit, as he that spake this day." Dimmesdale is not simply pale—"it seemed hardly the face of a man alive, with such a deathlike hue."

attention given to setting, the stationing of characters in the setting, gestures among characters, and dialogue. Throughout the scene, the action is heightened by the responses of the incredulous onlookers.

The action begins when Dimmesdale pauses and stretches out his hands to Hester and Pearl. In an obviously domestic touch, Pearl runs to Dimmesdale and throws her arms around his legs. Roger Chillingworth attempts to halt the action, but Dimmesdale repulses him. Dimmesdale ascends the scaffold and has important exchanges with the three main characters in his life—Hester, Pearl, and Chillingworth. Additionally, Dimmesdale makes a complete confession of his adultery and hypocrisy to the members of his church and community, identifying his sin as requiring God's forgiveness. At a climactic moment in the middle of all that is happening, Dimmesdale rips away his ministerial robe. In a touch of the supernatural, the narrator tells us that something was revealed, but it is left to our imaginations to guess what it is. At the very end of this packed action, Dimmesdale collapses in death.

Commentary

Chapter 23 is not simply the climax of *The Scarlet Letter*. It is one of the greatest pieces of imaginative writing ever produced. It is also what turns the story in a strongly Christian direction and in fact makes it a Christian classic. There is so much here that it is hard to know where to start unpacking it. One avenue is to explore Dimmesdale's interactions with the other characters (including the Puritan community as a group), starting with Chillingworth.

We might well have thought that in the previous chapter Hawthorne had done all with premonition that a storyteller could do, but he keeps the fireworks coming in the early part of this chapter. We read that Dimmesdale "had the foreboding of untimely death upon him." Again, "How feeble and pale he looked amid all his triumph." Throughout the sermon "there had been a certain deep, sad undertone of pathos, which could not be interpreted otherwise than as the natural regret of one soon to pass away."

Chillingworth's whole life had been built around manipulating Dimmesdale's guilt as a means of achieving revenge. He tries hard to maintain that control in this scene. Dimmesdale calls him a "tempter," and the satanic connection is reinforced when Chillingworth is repeatedly called "old." Chillingworth functions as an obstacle to Dimmesdale's conversion, and he admits defeat with the acknowledgment, "Thou hast escaped me."

Dimmesdale's interaction with Pearl, and her resulting development, are more complex. The key to what happens is that Dimmesdale acknowledges his father-child relationship for the first time. He invites Pearl with the words, "Come, my little Pearl," and she runs to him and clasps him by the knees. When Pearl kisses Dimmesdale's lips (and we remember her refusal to do so in the forest), "a spell was broken." The narrator calls what is happening "a great scene of grief," a moment that was anticipated in chapter 16 with the comment that Pearl lacked "a grief that should deeply touch her, and thus humanize and make her capable of sympathy." Here at the climax, "the wild infant" (Pearl's basic identity up to now) has "all her sympathies" unleashed, and henceforth "she would grow up amid human joy and sorrow, nor for ever do battle with the world, but be a woman in it."

Then there is Dimmesdale's changing relationship with the community. There is an element of rebuke when Dimmesdale announces, "People of New England, . . . ye, that have deemed me holy!—behold me here, the one sinner of the world!" Further, "There stood one in the midst of you, at whose brand of sin and infamy ye have not shuddered!" So the relationship between Dimmes-

"Hester is not the protagonist, the chief actor, and the tragedy of *The Scarlet Letter* is not her tragedy but Arthur's. He is the persecuted one, the tempted one. . . . His public confession is one of the noblest climaxes of tragic literature. . . . The confession was decisive. Its function in the novel is to resolve the action. It turned the scales in the great debate, though Hester, romantic heretic to the end, remained unconvinced, impenitent, unredeemed."
—Randall Stewart, *American Literature and Christian Doctrine*

dale and the community is one of new revelation and honesty.

God also enters the cast of characters in this great confession scene. Dimmesdale's references to God are conspicuous. To Chillingworth, Dimmesdale says, "With God's help, I shall escape thee now!" Earlier in the story Dimmesdale had been unable to move beyond seeing God as a God of judgment; now he says to Hester, "In the name of Him, so terrible and so merciful, who gives me grace, at this last moment, to do what—for my own heavy sin and miserable agony—I withheld myself from doing seven years ago." Again, "Thanks be to Him who hath led me hither!"

The references to God keep multiplying. The narrator claims that what is about to happen is "the judgment which Providence seemed about to work." Dimmesdale, we read, is about to "put in his plea of guilty at the bar of Eternal Justice." Regarding his sin, Dimmesdale says, "God's eye behold it!" For Hester and Pearl, says Dimmesdale, "be it as God shall order, . . . and God is merciful." Most climatically of all, Dimmesdale's last words in the whole book are a catalog of God's mercies, a biblical genre.

And there is, finally, the relationship between Hester and Dimmesdale that reaches its climax in this chapter. The main pattern is that Hester and Dimmesdale are foils to each other. We have noted the overwhelming degree to which Dimmesdale aligns himself with a Christian view of things. He believes that he has sinned and his sin needs to be forgiven by God. So he confesses and casts himself on God's mercy. His last words are as thoroughly Christian as words can be: "Had . . . these agonies been wanting, I had been lost for ever! Praised be

"Yet, all the time, Hawthorne means to reclaim Pearl from nature and to restore her to the jurisdiction of God and man. He clings to the notion that a child of God can return to God. . . . It is through Dimmesdale's expiation that Pearl becomes a human being. Her ultimate salvation rests with God, but her fate as a woman in this life lies in her father's hands. . . . Once the sin of her birth has been acknowledged, a psychic transformation overtakes her. When Dimmesdale reveals himself, the long search for the father is ended." —Chester E. Eisinger, "Pearl and the Puritan Heritage"

his name! His will be done! Farewell!" Dimmesdale embraces a Christian worldview, with forgiveness of sins as the highest value.

Hester has been the Romantic spokesperson
throughout the story, and she remains such in this
chapter. Dimmesdale, on the verge of the salvation of his soul, asks Hester, "Is not this better . . .
than what we dreamed of in the forest?" Hester
the Romanticist does not see it that way: "I know
not! I know not!" Hester the Romanticist wants
to believe that she and Dimmesdale will "spend
[their] immortal life together." She theorizes,
"Surely, surely we have ransomed one another,
with all this woe!" Dimmesdale's Christian reply
is, "Hush, Hester, hush! . . . The law we broke!—the
sin here so awfully revealed! . . . It may be, that,
when we forgot our God—when we violated our
reverence each for the other's soul—it was thence-
forth vain to hope that we could meet hereafter, in
an everlasting and pure reunion. God knows; and
He is merciful!"

The very last sentences of Dimmesdale's final,
farewell speech are particularly filled with theo-
logical and biblical meaning. After cataloging the
agonies that Dimmesdale paradoxically claims
were part of God's mercy to him, he asserts that
if any "of these agonies had been wanting, I had
been lost for ever." To be *lost* is a loaded theologi-
cal word that denotes being without salvation in
Christ and therefore to be condemned eternally
in hell. Dimmesdale's next statement is, "Praised
be his name." To *praise God's name* is a recurrent
formula in the Old Testament Psalms. And when
Dimmesdale follows that up with the declaration,
"His will be done," he repeats both a petition in the
Lord's Prayer (Matt. 6:10) and Jesus's resignation

"Hester Prynne, the
heroine of *The Scarlet
Letter*, typifies roman-
tic individualism, and
in her story Hawthorne
endeavored to exhibit
the inadequacy of
such a philosophy. . . .
Hester's apologists
unduly emphasize
circumstances which
seem to make her
the engaging central
figure of the romance,
and they ignore or
even decry the larger
tendency of the book
which subordinates
her and exposes her
moral inadequacy."
To excuse Hester "dis-
regards Hawthorne's
elaborate exposition
of the progressive
moral dereliction of
Hester. . . . Hawthorne
does feel moral
compassion for Hester,
but her role in the story
is to demonstrate that
persons who engage
our moral compas-
sion may nevertheless
merit moral censure."
—Darrell Abel,
"Hawthorne's Hester"

to the Father's will in his prayer in the garden of Gethsemane (Luke 22:42).

For Reflection or Discussion

This inspired piece of writing will repay all the time and mental energy that we invest in it. The exact sequence of events is important, so we need to analyze how one thing leads to another and how the overall Christian intention is structured. The skeleton on which Hawthorne arranged the data is the progress of Dimmesdale toward salvation, so it is important to isolate that story and see its contours all by itself. The logical next thing to do is look carefully at the developments that occur in the characters with whom Dimmesdale inter-acts—Chillingworth, the onlookers in the Puritan community, God, Pearl, and Hester. Finally, the chapter can be explored with a view toward delineating the Christian paradox around which Hawthorne weaves the action—Dimmesdale loses the world and gains his soul. Where do we see the outworking of what Dimmesdale himself para-doxically calls "a death of triumphant ignominy"?

Dimmesdale's final spoken words are, "Praised be his name! His will be done! Farewell." Literary critic Randall Stewart comments that "thus in his profoundest character-creation, and in the resolution of his greatest book, Haw-thorne has employed the Christian thesis: 'Father, not my will, but thine be done.'" —*American Literature and Christian Doctrine*

CHAPTER 24

Conclusion

Plot Summary

The plot was resolved at the end of the preceding chapter. The "conclusion" is a fireside chat with the author. The last phase of a plot is called *denoue-ment*—the tying up of loose ends. That is what happens in chapter 24 of *The Scarlet Letter*.

First Hawthorne takes up the question of

exactly what was revealed on the chest of Dimmesdale when he tore his ministerial garment away. Actually, all Hawthorne does is multiply alternate possibilities and leave the reader to choose among these theories. Then Hawthorne fills in the details of what happened to the other main characters. Chillingworth lost his purpose in life without Dimmesdale to torment; the only redeeming element in his characterization is that he left a large fortune to Pearl. Hester left the region temporarily and then returned to Boston, where she lived out her life. What happened to Pearl is left vague, but the suggestion is that she married an aristocrat in England and became a mother. When Hester died, she shared a tombstone with Dimmesdale, bearing the inscription, "On a field, sable [black], the letter A, gules [red]."

The most customary way for stories to end is with poetic justice: virtue is rewarded and vice is punished (Aristotle claimed that if a story does not end this way, our moral sense is not satisfied). The conventions of poetic justice governed Hawthorne's composition of chapter 24. Chillingworth's death within a year represents vice punished. Pearl's success is what we want for her. Hester has been a blend of the sympathetic and unsympathetic, and by the time we take into account everything that the narrator shares with us about her in chapter 24, we can see that a balance has been struck.

Commentary

The first important point to establish is that we should not try to make this the climax of the book. The great things have been completed by the end of the confession scene in chapter 23. Chapter 24 is not even packaged as "plot." It is a fireside chat with the author in which we learn about how three major actors reached their end.

Second, ending the story this way represents Hawthorne's adherence to a very strong convention in the novelistic tradition to end a novel on an upbeat note. Until the really pessimistic modern tradition became entrenched, the pressure was overwhelming for novelists to provide a happy ending for their stories. Even a pessimist such as Thomas Hardy tended to end his novels with something positive like a wedding. Chapter 24 of *The Scarlet Letter* gives us a modified happy end-

The Scarlet Letter narrates the effects of adultery, but the experience of adultery itself is not portrayed in the story. No adulterous emotions are described. Upon reflection here at the end of the story, though, we cannot help but feel deeply that all the sadness portrayed in the book was the result of an adulterous encounter and/or relationship. As we reach the close of the story, we cannot help but feel great regret that Hester and Dimmesdale committed adultery.

ing—certainly something more positive than we were expecting.

Within the parameter of the happy ending, Hawthorne does, however, preserve enough of the sadness of the story as a whole to make the final effect a balance among opposing moods. We are partly relieved to learn what happened to the other characters after Dimmesdale's death, but there are strong reminders of the overwhelmingly unhappy experiences that have been portrayed throughout the story. In particular, the final line of the book, which tells us about the inscription on the tombstone, strongly mitigates the sense of a happy ending that had been building up to that point in chapter 24.

For Reflection or Discussion

The overall task is to explore the ambivalence of the final chapter. The opening discussion of rival theories about what was revealed on Dimmesdale's chest shows this open-ended quality. After that, what positive things mitigate the sense of gloom that has overshadowed the story? Balancing that, what negative things temper any sense of a completely happy ending?

"We speak of a book as a classic when it has gained a place for itself in our culture, and has consequently become a part of our educational experience. But the term conveys further meanings implying precision of style [and] formality of structure. . . . Evaluated by these criteria, the list of unquestioned American classics is not a lengthy one. Often . . . it is headed by *The Scarlet Letter.*"—Harry Levin, "Introduction," *The Scarlet Letter*

Further Resources

The Scarlet Letter is one of the most written-about books in the whole realm of imaginative literature. Responses to it are varied and contradictory. With this work, particularly, it is crucial that readers not accept a viewpoint simply because a literary scholar has asserted it. A viewpoint is correct only if the text of *The Scarlet Letter* supports it.

Abel, Darrell. *The Moral Picturesque: Studies in Hawthorne's Fiction*, chaps. 14–18. West Lafayette, IN: Purdue University Press, 1988.

Baym, Nina. *The Scarlet Letter: A Reading*. Boston: G. K. Hall, 1986.

Fick, Leonard J. *The Light Beyond: A Study of Hawthorne's Theology*. Westminster, MD: Newman Press, 1955.

Gerber, John C., ed. *Twentieth-Century Interpretations of The Scarlet Letter*. Englewood Cliffs, NJ: Prentice-Hall, 1968.

Gross, Seymour L. *A Scarlet Letter Handbook*. San Francisco: Wadsworth, 1960.

Hawthorne, Nathaniel. *The Scarlet Letter*. Norton Critical Edition. Edited by Leland S. Person. New York: W. W. Norton, 2004.
    Numerous Norton Critical Editions of *The Scarlet Letter* from several editors have appeared through the years, all of them good.

Ryken, Leland. *Realms of Gold: The Classics in Christian Perspective*, chap. 6. Wheaton, IL: Harold Shaw, 1991.

Stewart, Randall. *American Literature and Christian Doctrine*. Baton Rouge, LA: Louisiana State University Press, 1958.

Glossary of Literary Terms Used in This Book

Apparent plot. The foreground or obvious line of action in a story, but by implication not the only line of action.

Character/characterization. The persons and other agents who perform the actions in a story.

Dramatic irony. A situation in which the reader knows something that one or more characters in the work of literature do not know.

Genre. Literary type or kind, like story or poem.

Guilty reader, technique of. A situation in which an author initially gets a reader to sympathize with a character or event and then later reveals the deficiencies and unsympathetic nature of that character or event.

Hidden plot. A line of the action in a story that requires careful scrutiny to discern; the "inside story" juxtaposed to what seems to be happening, possessing a degree of irony (based on a discrepancy between appearance and reality).

Narrative. Synonymous with *story*.

Plot. The carefully organized sequence of actions and events that make up a story, arranged as one or more conflicts that reach resolution.

Romance. Stories that include elements that are supernatural or marvelous rather than strictly realistic or lifelike.

Satire. A work of literature that exposes vice or folly.

Setting. The places where events in a story occur; can be temporal as well as physical.

Symbol/symbolism. A thing, person, or action that represents something in addition to itself; based on the principle of second meanings.

Symbolic reality. A situation in which there is such a preponderance of symbols in a text that what a reader chiefly encounters is a forest of symbols rather than literal things.

Theme. An idea about life that is embodied in a work of literature and that can be deduced from it.

HAWTHORNE'S
THE SCARLET LETTER

HOMER'S
THE ODYSSEY

MILTON'S
PARADISE LOST

SHAKESPEARE'S
MACBETH

Enjoy history's greatest literature with the aid of popular professor and author Leland Ryken as he answers your questions and explains the text.